— THE —

LinkedIn
CODE

Any queries relating to this publication or author may be sent to **info@topdogsocialmedia.com**

ISBN: 978-1499300468

Bulk discounts are available to use as promotions or for corporate LinkedIn and social selling training programs.

For details email is at: info@topdogsocialmedia.com

This book is also available in electronic format. Please visit **www.TopDogSocialMedia.com** for details.

— THE —
LinkedIn
CODE

Unlock The Largest Online Business Social Network To Get Leads, Prospects & Clients for B2B, Professional Services and Sales & Marketing Pros

MELONIE DODARO

Advance Praise For The LinkedIn Code

"If you are in business or you are in sales The LinkedIn Code is not an option, it's an imperative. This book covers every aspect of social selling and how you can use LinkedIn to your advantage. Don't just read this book, implement it."

Jeffrey Gitomer, New York Times best-selling author of
The Sales Bible & *The Little Red Book of Selling*

"Melonie's book is pure gold! It's like a powerful workshop in a book. If you're looking to finally get measurable results from your LinkedIn efforts, you must read The LinkedIn Code. Apply her proven step-by-step processes in this book and watch your results soar."

Mari Smith, author of *The New Relationship Marketing* & Coauthor
Facebook Marketing: An Hour A Day

"LinkedIn has been the most misunderstood and underrated social network. That changes as soon as you read *The LinkedIn Code*. Filled with practical advice and eye-opening tips, this is the "user's manual" for LinkedIn you'll wish you had years ago. Highly recommended."

Jay Baer, New York Times best-selling author of *Youtility*

"In *The LinkedIn Code*, Melonie Dodaro shares her method for abandoning the old ways of selling and embracing LinkedIn as a powerful tool to generate leads that lead to sales."

Michael Stelzner, CEO, Social Media Examiner, author of *Launch*

"How do you become a LinkedIn rainmaker? Melonie lays out how to best increase sales through best-of-breed LinkedIn approaches."

Robert Scoble, Rackspace's Startup Liaison Officer,
author *Age of Context*

"There's no denying that LinkedIn can be daunting to users. In *The LinkedIn Code*, Melonie Dodaro walks the reader through a logical step-by-step process of how to create a great profile and then use it to connect with ideal prospects and add more to your bottom line. This book is a fantastic guide to making LinkedIn work for you and your business!"

Joel Comm, New York Times best-selling author of
Twitter Power 2.0: How to Dominate Your Market One Tweet at a Time

"You don't have to be the smartest guy in the C-Suite to realize there's money to be made in social media. *The LinkedIn Code* gives you the secrets to cracking open the piggy bank."

Jeffrey Hayzlett, Primetime TV Host and C-Suite Executive

"*The LinkedIn Code* is, hands-down, the most articulate and professionally executed book of its kind. It shows you how to use LinkedIn to generate leads and attract all the clients you can handle. I would highly recommend this book as a valuable resource for anyone who wants to leverage LinkedIn to attract leads and grow their business."

Kim Garst, author of *Will The Real You Stand Up In Social Media*

"Melonie "knows" LinkedIn. She uses her extensive experience and expertise to take your social selling to the next level. This book is filled with easy to understand steps to help you get the most from LinkedIn."

Jeff Bullas, author of *Blogging The Smart Way*

Table of Contents

Preface

Being given a tool without some indication of what it is, how it works, why it works, and what happens when it is effectively put to work ensures that the tool will probably be set down. The potential user will go back to doing the work the same way it has always been done. I say this with confidence as I look at my bookshelf and see a number of professional how-to books that did not engage me past the preface or the introduction to the first chapter.

In exploring why, three things became evident. First, I was drawn to many of the books on my shelf because of the author or title. Second, I did not take the necessary time to evaluate whether my identified need was addressed by the purpose of the book or in the content developed for the author's "target audience". Third, despite a positive connection between the purpose of the book and my need, I wasn't necessarily committed to the work required to see the positive outcome I desired.

In order to support your success, I provide below a list of the "target audience" I believe will see the most benefit from my book here in the preface. Take a moment to review the list to see whether this book is ideal for you. I also lay out the purpose of the book and the strategies I will use to help you along the way.

The target audience includes:

- Professional Service Providers (e.g. attorneys, accountants, financial services)
- B2B[1] Sales Professionals & Sales Leaders
- B2B Business Owner

---

[1] B2B refers to business to business and B2C refers to business to consumer

- Coaches & Consultants
- Speakers & Authors
- Marketing Professionals
- Website Designers
- Graphic Designers
- Social Media Consultants
- Professional Writers
- Virtual Assistants
- Recruiters
- Anyone who wants to begin generating leads and sales using LinkedIn!

The purpose of my book is simple. I want to help you, and your business, successfully generate leads using the LinkedIn platform. To do this, I will share my knowledge and experience, industry best practices, relevant case studies, concept-driven exercises, and tools that can be practically and immediately applied. In essence, this book offers you the opportunity to practically apply what you read as you read it.

If, at this point you are seeing connections, identifying with the purpose of the book, and committed to doing the work ...

Let's get started!

Melonie Dodaro

Introduction

LinkedIn has completed its first decade, boasts over 300 million[2] global members and yet it is still viewed by many as a place to simply:

- post their resume

- seek endorsements (a form of reference) for their knowledge, skills, and abilities

- connect with old colleagues, classmates, or friends (using the platform in the same way they use Facebook or Twitter)

- recruit employees

What most people don't realize is that LinkedIn has the potential to allow its members to connect and build relationships with their ideal clients giving them un-gated access to the decision makers of their target companies.

According to a recent report released by LinkedIn [1]:

- One out of every three professionals in the world is on LinkedIn.

- LinkedIn is the #1 channel to distribute content.

- LinkedIn drives more traffic to B2B blogs and sites than other social media platforms.

- LinkedIn is considered the most effective social media platform for B2B lead generation.

The report goes on to state:

Since 2010, the number of B2B and B2C marketers generating sales via LinkedIn has grown consistently. U.S.-based agencies rate

---

[2] http://blog.linkedin.com/2014/04/18/the-next-three-billion/

LinkedIn as the most important social media platform for new business. In fact, 50% of our members report they are more likely to buy from a company they engage with on LinkedIn. And a whopping 80% of LinkedIn members want to connect with companies— because those connections provide them opportunities to enhance their professional decision-making. All it takes is a sophisticated marketer who seizes the opportunity to engage them.

While this statement certainly confirms my belief that LinkedIn is a powerful social selling[3] platform, I recognize that the effort required to become a "sophisticated marketer" might appear to be an overwhelming task to those looking at this lead generation strategy for the first time.

Based on my experience with both beginner and advanced users of LinkedIn, I have broken this book into two parts. This will make it easier to follow and implement.

Part one lays the foundation. In it, I will explain what social selling is, its growing significance as a marketing strategy, and why it will help you generate more leads. Then, I will focus on helping you to understand who your ideal clients are and the language they use. Next, I will help you create a professional and keyword-optimized LinkedIn profile, explain the 20 most important best practices on LinkedIn, and finish by explaining the social selling process.

In part two, we will create a lead generation campaign that you will use on LinkedIn. As part of this campaign, we will go through each of the activities that you will need to do on a daily, weekly, and monthly basis. I will also cover the reasons why you might consider upgrading to LinkedIn's premium services.

Finally, I will share with you a handy mnemonic[4] I created to help you remember everything you need to make LinkedIn a success for your business.

---

[3] Social Selling will be defined in the next chapter.
[4] Mnemonic - assisting or intended to assist memory, Merriam-Webster http://www.merriam-webster.com/dictionary/mnemonic

It's called the LinkedIn Code and will act as a review to help keep you on track when you are going through your daily checklist.

Throughout the book, I will provide you with a number of exercises and mini-worksheets to complete. You can complete some of the exercises right in the book, while others you may want to do in a word document on your computer or with a pen and paper. In some cases, such as when we go through how to create a professional and keyword optimized LinkedIn profile, you may want to work directly within LinkedIn as you read through each section.

Before we begin, I would like to share the story of Carol Montgomery with you. Carol's story will help you understand the power and potential of social selling on LinkedIn.

Social Selling Case Study 1 -
Carol Montgomery (VP Channels) of KnowBe4.com

www.linkedin.com/in/carolmontgomeryadams

Carol Montgomery began a new sales job last year for a security software company and found that email marketing and cold calls were not producing the kind of results she needed.

The Challenge

Most of Carol's leads were from the company website, non-paid organic searches, or incomplete and inaccurate lists. This resulted in a small percentage of A[5] leads and required a large amount of time to research each company. Determining which leads were within her target audience and which were not was an ineffective use of her time and resources.

---

[5] A leads are highly targeted and qualified leads

Carol needed a way to 1) eliminate wasted time and resources, and 2) increase her connection to high-level decision makers.

The Solution

Carol started to read Top Dog Social Media's blog[6] and Newsletter to learn about using LinkedIn as a lead generating sales strategy. She also decided to learn more about cold calling and email strategies from some "rapid fire cold callers"[7] she had met through one of her Channel Partners[8]. She then took the suggested cold calling phone and email scripts she got from these rapid fire cold callers and began to test the scripts against LinkedIn's connection requests. Carol found that LinkedIn proved to be a much more effective and time-efficient method for generating leads.

After taking the LinkedIn Profit Formula[9] course, Carol updated her LinkedIn profile so that it was professional and search friendly. She replaced the Google searches she had used in the past with LinkedIn searches to research companies, people and groups. Carol focused on executives in her target audience and created her own list of people to contact. To build her connection request messages, she used the relevant information she found on their LinkedIn profiles as well as the information she gleaned from the following:

- web searches

- company websites

- positioning statements, products and services, and press releases

Once she had a core list of about thirty to forty companies, including the names of various executives, she started sending connection requests and followed up each request with a phone call. If the connection request was not

---

[6] http://topdogsocialmedia.com/blog/
[7] "Rapid fire cold callers" are people who use RapidFire Cold Calling 3.0 for Appexchange by Salesforce.com
[8] "A channel partner is a company that partners with a manufacturer or producer to market and sell the manufacturer's products, services, or technologies. This is usually done through a co-branding relationship. Channel partners may be distributors, vendors, retailers, consultants, systems integrators (SI), technology deployment consultancies, and value-added resellers (VARs) and other such organizations." Wikapedia http://en.wikipedia.org/wiki/Channel_partner
[9] www.linkedinprofitformula.com

accepted within 48 to 72 hours, she would send another modified connection request, which was again followed up with a phone call.

When a request was accepted, she added them to a "Yes" list. She would then email them directly and call to set up an informational call.

Using this method, she cut her research time for leads in half and generated a much more targeted, results-producing lead list.

The Results

A week after beginning, she received a 15% response rate. After two weeks she had ten A leads with C-level executives[10] who were willing to have a brief conversation with her.

One of the leads turned out to be outstanding. When she called the CEO, the VP picked up the phone and said, "Hi Carol!" He had recognized her number from her contact information and continued the conversation with, "the CEO asked me to tell you we are interested, how about scheduling that chat?"

That one lead even asked Carol to introduce her company's product to their association of similar companies with 120 members. All of these companies were part of her target audience and potentially worth thousands of dollars in initial purchases and a recurring revenue stream for years to come.

Ultimately her A leads from LinkedIn were 300% above what she was generating from cold calling and email marketing. The conversion rate from these leads is now up to 35% and her ASP (Average Sales Price) has tripled.

Carol's pipeline has increased by 25% because LinkedIn allows her to connect directly with the executive level of her target audience faster and

---

[10] C-level or C-Suite generally refers to the top tier executives such as the chief executive officer (CEO), chief operations officer (COO), and chief financial officer (CFO).

easier than any other prospecting tool she has used. And because these leads were already at the C-level, it also cut her closing time in half.

Takeaways

Carol attributes her success, in connecting to prospects on LinkedIn, in large part to how she phrases her connection requests. She does not pitch her product, but instead asks for a mutual sharing of information about their respective companies. Carol finds that this works better than simply focusing on her company.

She also makes sure she does her homework beforehand by reading a prospects LinkedIn profile and going through the company's website to ensure that she has something meaningful to include in her connection requests and future messages with the potential prospect.

Carol states,

> *"LinkedIn is a powerful lead generation tool. Much better than Google or any other social media platform when used correctly."*

Part I

Laying the Foundation

Chapter 1: Social Selling

"Sellers who've embraced social media are creating new opportunities that totally bypass traditional sales channels....It's about good selling—using all the tools that are available to you today."
~Jill Konrath

Before we start to lay the foundation for your success with a great LinkedIn profile, I need to explain what social selling is and why LinkedIn is the best social media platform to use.

What is Social Selling?

Social selling refers to finding and connecting with potential prospects via social media to increase sales. Basically, social selling comes down to *building relationships* with potential prospects.

The Aberdeen Group [2] defines social selling as the utilization of one of the following three techniques:

1. **Social Collaboration:** sharing information internally or with partners to pool knowledge on how to generate more leads and sales.

2. **External Listening:** gathering and interpreting information or content produced by clients and prospects.

3. **External Participation:** providing prospects with relevant and helpful content or information to build relationships and positively impact future buying decisions.

Consider for a moment the effectiveness of cold calls and emails. On average, two hundred emails will flood your prospect's inbox every day—

most of them are unwanted. Now factor in that over 90% of decision makers state that they absolutely will not buy from a cold call or an unsolicited email. [3] This paints a pretty bleak outlook for the current sales and marketing endeavors of many companies.

While you may have a hard time reaching your prospects or target market using more traditional marketing methods, new methods such as social selling are proving very effective. Keep in mind that 82% of your prospects can be reached socially via online networks and these same decision makers are using social networks, such as LinkedIn, to research and exchange information on vendors and their products or services. In fact, a 2012 survey [4] found that 77% of B2B buyers did not speak with a salesperson until after they had performed independent research.

Whether we like it or not, social selling is happening. It is happening in every industry and in all corners of the world. The reality is that someone is educating and providing insight with helpful content to your prospects and clients. Your prospects will ultimately take the path of least resistance and choose to use the company that has been helping them along their buying journey. The question is, when your prospects are searching, will it be you or your competitors that they find?

If you're still not convinced of the power of social selling to generate more leads and clients, consider that 72.6% of salespeople who use social media outperform their colleagues who aren't using it. [5] In fact, The Aberdeen Group [2] has collected some powerful statistics that provide compelling evidence about the benefits of social selling. These statistics suggest that top social selling businesses and sales teams:

- were 36% more likely than the average business or sales team to achieve their quota
- saw a 12.2% higher year-over-year increase in total company revenue than the average business or sales team.

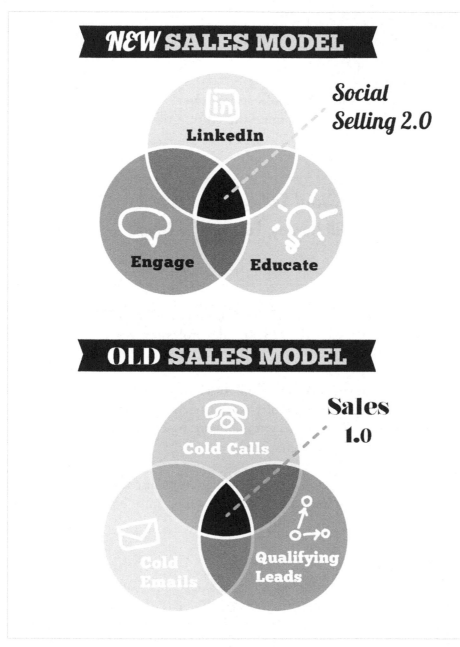

Image 1.1: The old versus the new sales model.

Social selling is currently producing amazing results for B2B companies, professional service providers, and marketing and sales professionals in every industry all over the world.

Below is a case study that looks at how Oracle, under the training of Jill Rowley, has begun to incorporate the culture of social selling into their company.

Social Selling Case Study 2 –
Jill Rowley, Formerly of Oracle

www.linkedin.com/in/jillrowley

Oracle is a company that has recognized the power of social selling and has begun training their more than 23,000 sales professionals to use social selling. Jill Rowley took on the challenge of training the sales team.

Once a sales professional herself, Jill Rowley was known for being a "quota crushing" sales rep during the fifty-two quarters she worked for Salesforce.com and Eloqua. When Eloqua was purchased by Oracle, Jill went on to train Oracle's sales team for over ten months.

Jill is now an independent social selling evangelist and consultant who aims at transforming the world of social selling into "social serving" one company at a time.

The Challenge

Set with the task of training 23,000 Oracle sales professionals around the world on how to social sell, Jill was faced with no budget, no staff, and a company that was deeply rooted in using old sales techniques.

Her first, and possibly most difficult, challenge was to ensure that the sales professionals understood the changes that had taken place in the B2B buyer and buying process. Buyers today are very different than they were just ten years ago.

She needed to teach Oracle's sales professionals to "stop selling and start serving."

The Solution

Jill knew that in order to be successful, she had to help Oracle's sales professionals understand why it was in their best interests to learn the social selling process. She needed to help them understand that today's buyers are mobile, digitally driven, and socially connected with the ability to access real-time information to educate themselves about any given product.

She taught Oracle's sales professionals that in order to thrive in today's marketplace, they needed to start using the social networks their buyers were using. Jill explained how the sales professionals could use these social networks to do research, to network, to share useful content, and to build relationships. The sales professionals realized they needed to use these social networks to earn a buyer's trust, regardless of whether the buyer purchased from the salesperson or not.

Once the sales team understood why social selling was vital, Jill created an online social selling curriculum with the Oracle Sales Academy. Each training video taught viewers a social selling skill or tool. She hired an outside firm to help her create the content that would be used for training. She reviewed their content, picked out what was most applicable and then modified, enhanced, and branded it to suit Oracle's specific needs in Oracle's training studio.

Results

Oracle's sales team responded well to the training. Jill received daily invites to connect on LinkedIn from Oracle sales reps complimenting, congratulating, and thanking her for her training.

She has helped Oracle's sales professionals deepen their relationships with their customers, partners, and other stakeholders, leading to higher wallet share and higher revenue for the company.

Takeaways

Jill believes that part of the challenge with the term "social selling" is the fact that the word "selling" is in the term. Modern sales professionals don't sell, they serve, help, and educate. But before sales reps can really excel at social selling, they have to have that "aha" moment, in order to shift their mindset and understand why it is so important.

She states that,

> *"If you just look at the data, 92% of B2B buyers start their search on the web, and 82% of the world's online population can be reached via social networks. You can't afford not to make time for social selling."*

While adopting this new frame of mind will be especially challenging for larger companies like Oracle, it will become increasingly important if they are to remain competitive in their market. Jill shares,

> *"It's not an easy thing to change deep-rooted cultural values and to become a social business. The culture has to be one of transparency, collaboration, and real time engagement. Engagement needs to occur on the networks where your customers are. And it needs to occur without sales personnel having to go through a scripted, lengthy,*

legal PR review process to be able to say anything publicly."

Jill developed a method called the "5 Step Framework to Design, Deploy & Drive Adoption of Social Selling" to help train the team. The five steps are:

1. Help sales people create their personal brand.

2. ABC = Always Be Connecting. Socially surround the buyer, buying committee, and their sphere of influence.

3. Content is the currency of the modern sales professional.

4. Social listening for leads.

5. Measure what matters.

Social Selling on LinkedIn

Some of the greatest social selling successes to date have been achieved using LinkedIn. In fact, LinkedIn has been shown to be 277% more effective for lead generation than either Facebook or Twitter, even though most people are not using LinkedIn to its full potential. [6]

The reason that LinkedIn is so powerful is not only because its members include one third of all professionals in the world or that all of the Fortune 1000 companies are represented, but also because the platform is designed to help you *build relationships* with your contacts. In Part 2, I will share the numerous features and tools that LinkedIn offers its members to help them interact regularly and meaningfully with their contacts.

But before we move on to defining your ideal clients (Chapter 2), I want to share with you another social selling case study. This one is the story of Scott Logan [7], who achieved great success for his company through social selling on LinkedIn.

Social Selling Case Study 3 –
Scott Logan of inContact

www.linkedin.com/in/scottjlogan

Before using social selling, Marketing Campaign Manager Scott Logan and his sales team from inContact used popular lead generation tactics for sales teams. These included sending out regular emails then following up on inbound leads via phone as well as cold calling.

The Challenge

Over time Scott started to notice that his team's email efforts were not producing the result they once had. They were increasingly challenged with finding true qualified leads, being able to reach the decision makers, and connecting with decision makers without annoying them.

The Solution

Scott decided to do some research. He looked at a variety of information that he found online as well as a slideshow called *The Evolution of LinkedIn* [8] and discovered something called social selling. This piqued his interest. The more research he did, the more he realized the powerful potential of social selling and LinkedIn.

Scott knew that he needed to be ahead of the game and get a handle on the concept and process of social selling. He also knew that he had to have a well-documented reporting process showing a clear ROI. Scott created a social selling process from scratch using the results of his research and the AB split test[11] described next.

---

[11] AB Split Testing refers to simple random experiments with two variants, A the control and B the treatment in the experiment.

At the time only half of his team (A) had a complete and professional looking LinkedIn profile and made use of it for the purpose of networking. He trained this group on social selling, which they then put into practice. The other half of his team (B) continued to use their current sales and marketing practices. He then implemented a method of tracking that would show lead sources and identify differences between the reps using social selling and those that were not.

The Results

Within three months of being trained, group (A) implementing social selling techniques had a 160% bigger sales pipeline than group (B) using traditional methods of marketing and selling.

Seeing the success of their peers, the rest of Scott's team started to adopt the basics of social selling. Those who continued to grow their social selling expertise over the following nine months realized 215% more revenue in their pipeline by the end of 2013.

Today, Scott's sales team is connecting, via LinkedIn, with everyone in their pipeline. They recognize the importance of building the relationship regardless of whether a prospect is ready to purchase at the time or not. Through the regular sharing of quality content and consistent nurturing of relationships, they have become and continue to stay top of mind. Social selling techniques are now a part of inContact's sales organization's DNA and have been included in their annual sales kick-off conference.

Social Selling has allowed Scott and his team to broaden inContact's exposure to a larger audience as well as zero in on prospects based on their location. For example, his team, as part of a 25 city regional outreach, host a 90-minute panel discussion over lunch with a series of experts in specific locations across the US and Canada. To initially connect with these prospects, they use regional LinkedIn groups (city, state, or provincial groups for example) to invite them to the training. 42% of all registrations for each event come from connecting within those regional LinkedIn groups.

Takeaway

There exists an abundance of evidence suggesting that if used effectively, social selling in general and LinkedIn specifically, will generate leads and increase revenue. This is not meant to suggest that traditional marketing practices should be discarded like the proverbial baby with the bathwater. One of the greatest benefits of social selling is that it doesn't disrupt or replace existing marketing and sales processes (unless it is meant to). Social selling will actually enhance a company's existing practices.

In addition, it will augment those areas where sales processes aren't currently focused. For example, social selling is ideal for the pre-qualification stage to find and connect with brand new prospects, bringing new leads into the pipeline that wouldn't have existed without its use.

Scott states in his training that social selling eliminates the *gatekeeper*[12]. Reaching decision-makers is easier than ever. If the social seller is seen to be a field expert, keeper of knowledge, and a resource, the decision-maker is more likely to allow unfettered access. As such, the only thing that would stand between the social seller and decision-maker is a lack of relevant content to share or the inability of the social seller to effectively communicate it.

Scott [7], in explaining why he and his team will continue to use social selling and the LinkedIn platform states:

> *"It is a long-term process, however, the reps that use it see immediate results. Soon social selling will be the standard so you want to ensure that you are embracing this now."*

---

[12] You can send a connection request or InMail directly to any LinkedIn member, regardless of who they are or what position they hold.

inContact is the cloud contact center software leader, helping organizations around the globe create high quality customer experiences. To learn more, visit **www.incontact.com** or follow the conversation on **Twitter** or **Facebook**.

Chapter 2: Defining Your Ideal Client

"Everyone is not your customer."
~ Seth Godin

In the last chapter you learned that the power behind successful social selling is the relationship that you build with your prospects. Before we explore how best to do that, it is important that you first determine who you want to market to. There are a number of questions you will want to answer up front.

- Who is your ideal client?

- What is the common language of his or her business, industry, or organization?

- What kinds of challenges does he or she face?

Egoic Labels

Steve Olsher [9] states that, "Profitability depends on delivering pertinent content and desired solutions to a specific audience." When this statement and the quote that begins this chapter are taken together, a common message is revealed—*one size does not fit all.* Even though you may be seeking prospects within a specific industry (where some generalities may be made), you are dealing with individuals. At the end of the day, it is not the industry, business, or organization you will be building the relationship with, you will be building a relationship with the individuals who make the decisions.

This is why we begin our discussion about implementing social selling with the client. Your LinkedIn profile must be 100% client focused. In order to ensure that this is the case, the first step requires that you get a clear picture of who your ideal client is.

When we ask people how they see themselves, they would probably give a number of different answers depending on where, when, and how we ask the question. Their description might focus on their profession, educational status, nationality, relationship status, gender, religion, recreational activities, or volunteer activities. They may also use descriptors such as successful businessperson, strong leader, money-saving accountant, profitable business owner or awesome speaker.

Exercise 1

Take a moment right now and think about how you would describe yourself to me if I asked. Think broadly (you can use the categories previously mentioned) and come up with as many labels as you can. Note how many of the labels are personal and how many are professional.

In completing the short exercise above, you have developed what is called a list of *egoic* labels. Egoic labels refer to those terms we use to describe ourselves to others. Egoic labels can change due to the passage of time as well as changes in a person's professional or personal life. What remains constant is that egoic labels convey what is most meaningful to us about who we are personally, and what we do professionally.

For example, a woman who is also a mother will almost always identify herself first as a mother (an intrinsically and socially strong egoic label). Some business owners might identify themselves as a business owner, while others might call themselves an entrepreneur or simply describe themselves by the service they provide. Your relationship building will fall short if you don't understand the nuances of the egoic labels used by your prospects.

Exercise 2

For this exercise I want you to write your answers in as much detail as you can. The goal is to know your ideal clients so well that you can think like them, speak like them, experience their emotions, and essentially *be* those clients.

I can almost hear you groan. Perhaps you're looking about to see if anyone will catch you should you decide to just skip this and the next couple of exercises and move on to the meat of the book. I can sympathize. What I am asking is difficult for most people to do. But, I want you to remember that we are laying the foundation for your success. While you may not see the relevance yet, you certainly will by the end of the book. Let's begin shall we.

Think about your top ten clients[13]. Based on what you know about them, I would like you to identify some general commonalities and differences between them. You can sort them, for example, by looking at role, demographics, industry or organization, region served, personal traits, and leadership or management style.

---

[13] If you are just starting you might want to Google companies and organizations in your field of interest and read the bios of their senior administration.

_____

_____

_____

_____

_____

_____

_____

_____

_____

_____

_____

_____

_____

_____

_____

_____

_____

_____

Narrowing your focus, I would next like you to construct a list of possible egoic labels for each of your top ten clients. Again, make note of the commonalities and differences. For example are your ideal clients technology companies, HR directors, accountants, etc.

1. _____

2. _____

3. _____

4. _____

5. _____

6. _____

7. _____

8. _____

9. _____

10. _____

Exercise 3

Next, take a walk in their shoes and look at life through their eyes.

The Fears of Your Ideal Clients

Answer the following questions as if you were your ideal client. Don't hold back!

What do you worry about? What keeps you up at night?

_____

_____

_____

What do you not look at because it triggers too much fear?

_____

_____

_____

What is the worst case scenario for your business?

_____

_____

_____

What is a worst case scenario for your business that is FAR worse than your current worst case scenario?

_____

_____

_____

Where will you lose power, influence, and control in your life if things don't change or get worse?

_____

_____

_____

The Hopes of Your Ideal Clients

Now let's dive into your client's perfect scenarios. This is what your client hopes for the most.

What do you secretly wish was true about your business situation?

_____

_____

_____

What is the dream solution for your business that you would pay almost anything for?

_____

_____

_____

If your perfect dream solution happened, how would that look?

_____

_____

_____

How will others respond to you if your fantasy situation comes true?

_____

_____

_____

What will you be able to do, get, or achieve if your fantasy situation comes true?

_____

_____

_____

Where will you be more powerful and influential in your life if your fantasy situation comes true?

_____

_____

_____

Exercise 4

Now that you've spent some time in your client's shoes, it's time to go deeper and be even more specific. You have just provided the solution for an issue challenging your client[14]. What primary emotion or set of emotions is your ideal client feeling at the exact moment the client is buying your product or service? What is going through your client's mind? What specific words does your client use as he or she thinks about you, your service, or product, and the potential results your client will see because of your help.

Write everything down that comes to mind from the perspective of your client. Writing **AS** your client allows you to include what the client might be thinking but would never say out loud to you.

_____

_____

_____

_____

_____

[14] The term "client" is meant to represent both "client" and "customer" in this book.

It's All About the Language

One of the biggest mistakes marketers can make is to use language that represents their creativity rather than the language used by their clients. It is essential that you do your homework and speak the language that your ideal clients use.

Using the same language that your ideal clients use is incredibly important for two reasons. For one thing, if your keywords do not match the terms that your clients use in searches, they will not be able to find you.

For example, let's say you're a branding consultant and you describe yourself (egoic label) as a *branding expert*. Your ideal clients however, when searching for a branding consultant, use the keywords *marketing consultant* or *marketing expert*. As a result, they do not find you in their search.

The second reason is that what you put on your profile must resonate with your potential clients when they find you or they will keep looking for someone else who does.

Let me share an example of what I mean. First, imagine you're a business coach, and you want to work with clients who are looking for ways to grow their business and make more money. You begin to think about your approach and the marketing message you will create to attract clients. Which of the following two options do you think prospects might be more likely to respond to?

1. Are you seeking more abundance and financial freedom?

2. Are you a business owner looking to attract more clients and make more money?

The best way to know the words and phrases your ideal clients use is to:

- listen to the language used by your current ideal clients
- pay attention to the language used when a prospect approaches you to learn more about what you have to offer
- use the answers to the questions asked by your prospects

Being aware of the words and phrases commonly used by your ideal clients is very important because those are the keywords you'll be using to optimize and strengthen your LinkedIn profile.

Takeaways

The widespread and growing recognition in business that, "it's not what you know but who you know" strongly indicates that one of the keys to being successful is the development of relationships. The best way to ensure that you are connecting with your ideal clients and building relationships that will increase your success (and theirs) is to take the time to know who they are, the language they use, and the challenges they face.

In addition, defining your ideal clients is the first step in laying the foundation for a powerful LinkedIn profile. Be sure to complete the exercises above and then join me in Chapter 3 to begin crafting a powerful LinkedIn profile.

Chapter 3: Creating a Great LinkedIn Profile

"The aim of marketing is to know and understand the customer so well the product or service fits him and sells itself."
~Peter Drucker

Having a professional and search-optimized profile is essential to your success on LinkedIn. In fact, I highly recommend that you don't start actively using LinkedIn as a lead generation or business building tool until you have done this.

In this chapter, I am going to take you step-by-step through every aspect of your LinkedIn profile to make sure it is optimized well, looks professional, and most of all, is client-focused. In other words, your profile speaks to who your ideal clients are and how you can help them.

LINKEDIN PRO TIP

Before you begin making changes to your LinkedIn profile, especially if you're doing a complete revamp, it is **essential** that you turn off your *Notifications*.

You do this by **unchecking** the *Turn on/off your Activities Broadcast* box in the *Privacy & Settings* section and then saving the changes.

If you skip this step, your connections will be notified every time you make a change. You don't want to inundate your network with each and every change you make to your profile so uncheck that box before you do anything else.

Keywords

The first step in creating a great profile is to choose the right keywords. If potential clients are looking on LinkedIn for the products or services you offer and you're not showing up in their search, that's a lost opportunity. To make sure you show up in their search, you need to choose the right keywords and put them in the right places—this is what is meant by *optimizing your profile*.

There is a difference between choosing keywords so that you will be found on LinkedIn and choosing keywords for your website so that you can be found through a Google search. The core difference is that with a Google search, people are typically looking for things or information, whereas on LinkedIn, they are looking for a person who provides a particular service or product.

Example 1:

If someone is looking for information on how to create a great LinkedIn profile on Google, the person might search using the keywords, *how to create a LinkedIn profile*.

If someone is looking for a person to teach him or her how to create a great LinkedIn profile or even write a great LinkedIn profile, the person might search using keywords such as, *LinkedIn expert, LinkedIn consultant, LinkedIn trainer*.

People will often look for title-based keywords on LinkedIn.

Example 2:

Let's say you are an accountant or a business coach. Those words are titles, rather than the services you offer. So on LinkedIn, instead of using the keyword *accounting service*, as you might on Google, use the keyword *accountant*. Instead of saying *business coaching*, say *business coach*.

Your Profile Headline

Your next step is to create a compelling and search-optimized LinkedIn headline. Your headline is the *MOST* important part of your profile.

What is a headline? Where is it found?

Optimize your headline (see image 3.1) with at least one or two keywords. This carries a lot of weight in LinkedIn's algorithm causing your profile to show up at the top of the search results.

Of course, it is not enough to simply show up in the search results because many other profiles will as well. In order to stand out, you should also ensure that your headline includes a statement that captures your readers' attention and intrigues them enough to want to click on your profile.

You **only have 120 characters**, and I suggest you use them all to insure your profile is click worthy.

Contact Information

Next, you need to update your contact information. Make sure you include your email, your phone number, and any other information you want people to see.

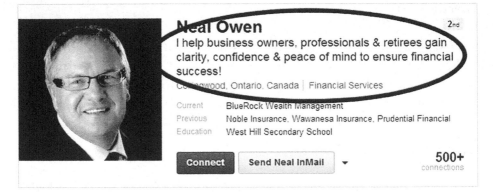

Image 3.1: Create a headline that is compelling and keyword optimized.

Vanity URL

By default, LinkedIn will create a URL for you. The URL will include your first name, dot, last name, forward slash, a series of numbers with a dash, and another string of numbers.

You need to change the URL you are given to what's known as a *Vanity URL* (see Image 3.2). If at all possible, you should select your name for your vanity URL. If your name is not available, try putting in a middle initial, or a designation at the end.

LINKEDIN PRO TIP

I caution you not to use your company name here, because this is your *Personal Profile*. There is no guarantee that you will own or work for the same business in the future, but your name will still be your name. So secure your personal name.

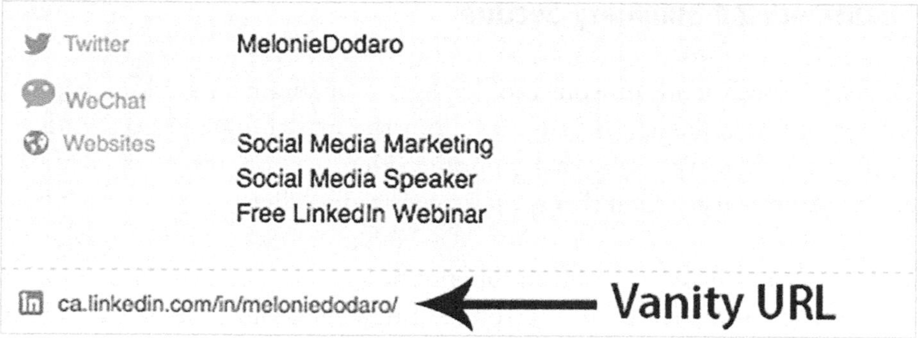

Image 3.2: Set your vanity URL as your name if possible.

Your Website

In your contact information, you can include your website. LinkedIn's default label for this is *company website*, or *company blog*. But you can and should customize it.

This is another opportunity for keyword optimization. You can choose to use specific keywords, or you might use your company name. In my own case, (see Image 3.2), I use the keywords *social media marketing*, but I could also use my company name, *Top Dog Social Media*.

LinkedIn gives you three spots, so if you have more than one website, include up to three of them here. If you only have one website, you can still take advantage of all three. For example, you might set one to go to your home page, one to a service page, and perhaps one to a download you are offering. This will encourage people to visit those pages where you can provide them with more information about your business offerings.

Client-Focused Summary Section

Once somebody lands on your profile page, your summary section becomes tremendously important because it's often the first thing a person reads to learn more about you and what you offer. Here are some ways to create an effective summary section that speaks to your ideal client.

- Your LinkedIn profile should not be a job resume that's written with you as the focus. The person reading your profile doesn't care about what awards you've won and what sales records you've broken. The truth is that nobody cares about you — they care about what you can do for them. So make sure your summary is client-focused.

- Write the summary in the first person. Even though it is business-oriented, LinkedIn is still a *social* network, so don't forget to be social! One way to do this is to write in the first person, not in the third person.

- Speak directly to your target market. When they land on your profile, you want your potential clients to know they're in the right place and that you are the person who can help them with their specific problems. You will also want to include your chosen keywords in your summary section.

Your summary can be **up to 2,000 characters**, and again, I suggest you use them all. I have created a three-part formula to craft a compelling and client focused summary.

1. Credibility Section

2. Ideal Clients—Their Problem—Your Solution

3. Call to Action

First, start with your **credibility section.** This should contain one or two

Background

Summary

When social media was just getting started I was searching for the best tools to promote my book and discovered social media as the perfect tool. Social media is a powerful platform for business, WHEN USED PROPERLY!

For years I studied everything I could about online marketing and SOCIAL MEDIA. Over time I became the "Go-To" leading authority on social media and opened my social media agency Top Dog Social Media. I've worked with the world's leading experts and have been dubbed by the media as Canada's #1 LINKEDIN EXPERT & social media strategist.

I'm passionate about helping my clients use social media marketing STRATEGICALLY. Those that want to learn about social media go to Google. Those who want RESULTS with social media...come to us.

Here's who we work with:

✓ BRANDS & BUSINESSES - Are you looking to maximize your online activities to increase visibility and profitability? We create custom SOCIAL MEDIA STRATEGIC PLANS that align with your goals. We can do the implementation for you if you want to leave it to the experts!

✓ VP of SALES or SALES MANAGERS - Does your sales force ever struggle to achieve their sales goals? We can teach them highly effective SOCIAL SELLING techniques to generate warm leads, more sales & exceed their sales quota.

✓ PROFESSIONALS & ENTREPRENEURS - Would you like to build your personal brand, INFLUENCE, IMPACT & INCOME? We can help you to be seen as the #1 leading EXPERT in your niche and/or community in as little as 6 months!

✓ CONFERENCE & EVENT PLANNERS, ASSOCIATIONS & FRANCHISORS - Are you looking for a Keynote Speaker [Social media speaker, LinkedIn Speaker] that will educate & inspire your delegates on social media, social selling or influence marketing? I offer engaging & custom presentations to fit your audience!

►If you're interested in Social Media Marketing Services, Social Selling Training, LinkedIn Campaigns that produce massive results or having me speak at your event, email me at: info@TopDogSocialMedia.com

Click to PLAY VIDEO - Are you wasting time with social media? Click to find out how to get results!

Click to PLAY VIDEO if you're looking for a Social Media Keynote Speaker for your event!

Image 3.3: Your Summary section must speak to your ideal clients.

short paragraphs which will tell prospective clients a little bit about: who you are, your story, why you do what you do, and your background. Be sure to mention anything to enhance your credibility such as media attention, publications, well-known clients, years of experience, or anything else that makes you stand out. This establishes your credibility for what you do.

Next, identify your **ideal clients.** This will allow prospective clients to recognize themselves and to know they are in the right place. This is where the egoic labels we covered earlier become vital. You identify the types of clients you work with and then speak directly to them about **their problems** and **your solutions** to those problems.

Essentially, you want to ensure that once your ideal clients land on your profile, they will self-select themselves after realizing that you are someone they need to connect with.

Finally, you should have a clear **call to action**—tell prospective clients exactly what you want them to do next. Do you want them to pick up the phone and call you? Do you want them to email you? Tell them what they need to do.

Example: My Summary Section

Let's use my Summary Section (See Image 3.3) as an example of how I put the three-part formula into practice. In my **credibility** section, I tell viewers:

- a little bit about me and my story
- how I got involved with social media
- how I opened up my social media agency
- how I became what the media calls Canada's No. 1 LinkedIn Expert
- how I help the clients I work with

In my **client-focused** section, I speak directly to my ideal clients. I identify them using egoic labels, acknowledge the needs and or issues of each label, and then provide my solutions for each. So, if any Vice Presidents for Sales land on my profile, they will see right away that I am speaking to them—I've identified them, the problem their sales teams have, and my solution of using social selling training to increase their leads and sales conversions.

I close with my call to action, telling them what I want them to do.

"If you're interested in learning more about how I can help you with social media or social selling or having me speak at your next event email me at info@TopDogSocialMedia.com."

If you miss this part, as most people do, then you leave it to chance that they will actually follow up. People often have the best of intentions and plan to follow up but then forget. So tell them exactly what to do and help them take that action now.

Current Work Experience

This describes what you're doing right now in your business or your current position. It is also another opportunity to include your keywords in your title and your description. Just like the Summary section, you have **2000 characters to describe your current work experience**, so make sure you make full use of them.

If you have more than one business or more than one focus within your business, you can actually create two current work experience sections. This is what I have done as I have experience in two separate areas. My first work experience section talks about my agency, *Top Dog Social Media*, what we do, and who we are. The second section talks about my experience as a keynote speaker on how to use LinkedIn and social selling. This section mentions the various presentations that I do. If you have two businesses, markets, or focuses, you can do it this way as well.

The formula you use for your current work experience is similar to how you laid out your summary, but with some minor differences.

First, begin with your company credibility section. This is where you talk about the company you work for or the company you own. Share the most compelling information about your company here.

I recently worked with a company that has been operating for more than one hundred years, and nowhere in the company profile or on any of the employee profiles does it say that! I stumbled upon this information on the company's website. But this is huge! How many companies have been open for more than a hundred years? That's a powerful piece of information that will increase a company's credibility and it should absolutely be added to the work experience description.

Next you can list all of the services you provide. This is another good spot for keyword optimization.

There are a couple of optional things you might consider adding to your current work experience. The first one is a list of current and past clients. If you have well-known clients or brands you've worked with that your ideal client would recognize, include their names. If they're not well-known brands, you can simply list the types of clients you work with. For example, you might say, "I work with accounting and law firms."

Another possibility is to add one powerful client testimonial. If you have a great client testimonial on your website that isn't shown as a recommendation on your LinkedIn profile, you can include it here.

Lastly, in your current work experience description, include a call to action. You can use the same call to action that you created in the summary section and add it to the bottom of your description section.

Rich Media

LinkedIn has an amazing rich media feature that allows you to add videos, slideshows, and PDFs. Adding multimedia to your summary and current work experience sections makes your profile look more visually appealing and provides your readers with another way to engage with the message you are sharing.

A video might welcome visitors to your profile or teach them something that will be beneficial to them and their business. It could also be a company video, a corporate video, or a testimonial video. PDFs can be articles, white papers, or a brochure describing your products or services. Great slideshow examples can include presentations you've delivered or be a more visual way to deliver any content you might want to share. If you do add multimedia, be sure the content is both professional in appearance and relevant.

Click to PLAY VIDEO - Are you wasting time with social media? Click to find out how to get results!

Click to PLAY VIDEO if you're looking for a Social Media Keynote Speaker for your event!

Image 3.4: Add multimedia to your profile to make your profile more interactive.

LINKEDIN PRO TIP

You can add videos while you are editing your profile by checking the little box with a plus (+) symbol. This button allows you to add a link. You can add a link from YouTube or anywhere else there is a video you want to include. The video will automatically pop up on your profile.

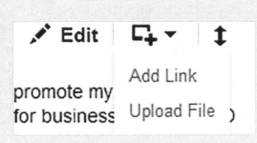

Image 3.5: Add a video to your profile by clicking the box with a plus symbol and selecting Add Link.

It's a good idea to customize the text so that your readers will know that the link goes to a video. You should also provide a brief description of what the video or multimedia content is about to encourage people to click on it.

To upload PDFs and other documents, simply click *upload file*, then choose the file from your computer and upload it into your profile.

Past Experience

Your past experience doesn't need to be as comprehensive as your current experience, but should at least include a paragraph describing relevant past experience so that your profile looks complete.

Skills

You can include up to 50 skills on your profile. You should include all of your keywords as well as a list of your actual skills and the services you offer. Over time, people will start endorsing you for these skills. I suggest you add at least ten skills as that is the number that is prominently displayed showing the endorsements you've received.

There is evidence that shows the more endorsements you have for a specific skill, the better the positioning of that term in LinkedIn search results.

Volunteer Experience, Causes, Organizations

Your volunteer experience should go in this section. Make sure that you add all of your volunteer experience in this section.

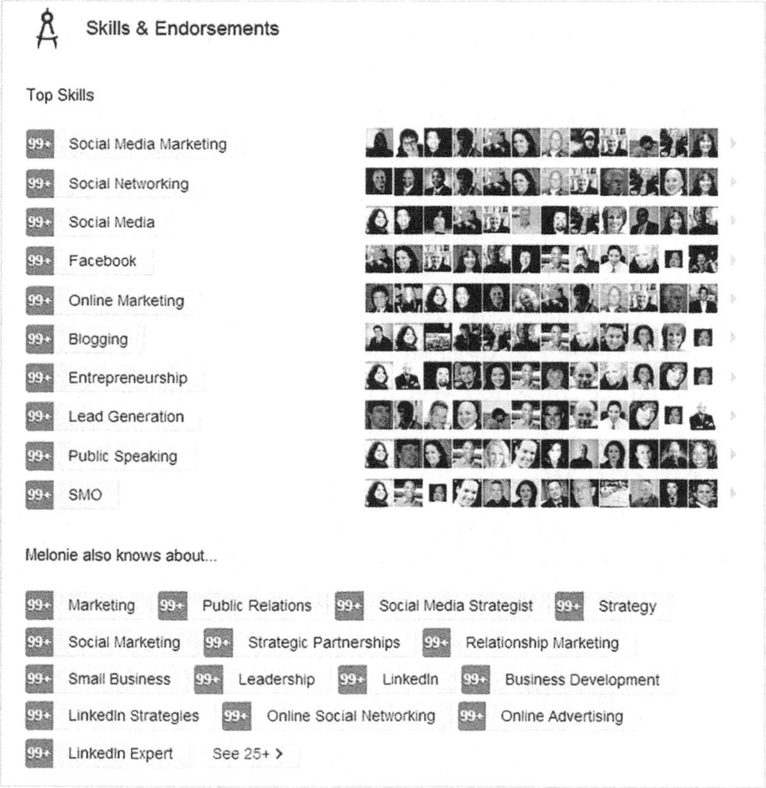

Image 3.6: You can add and be endorsed for up to 50 skills.

LINKEDIN PRO TIP

The volunteer experience section isn't a default section within your profile—you actually have to add it manually.

In addition to listing your volunteer experience, you will find the **causes you care about** area. Be sure to take the time to select the causes that are important to you.

Within this section, you can also add the **organizations you support** with either your time, money, or your energy. Identifying the causes and organizations you support will tell your readers a little more about you, and just as importantly, allow them to connect with you in one more way.

Education

Now you need to complete your education section. This is very basic and easy to do. Simply insert your post-secondary education in this section. There is also an additional section where you can add your certifications.

LINKEDIN PRO TIP

If you want to add the certification section to your profile, you'll need to manually add this just as you did with your volunteer experience.

Additional Information

You should complete the **Interests** section that is found within the Additional Information section as well as provide advice on how your readers can contact you. It is, however, optional whether you want to include your birthday or marital status.

LINKEDIN PRO TIP

Insert a couple of your **keywords** in the Interests section. You can also include both personal and professional interests. Include your **call to action** from the Summary section in the Advice for Contacting section.

Honors and Awards

You can add an Honors and Awards section to your profile and list anything for which you've received awards, honors, or accolades. You can also list any media attention you've received. If you don't have relevant information for this section, simply leave it out of your profile.

Recommendations

Finally, I strongly advise that you get recommendations on your profile as this provides important social proof. When people are deciding who to do business with, they are often swayed by the decisions others have made, so the more recommendations you have the better. But this doesn't mean that you have to go and get a huge number of recommendations. Shoot for five to ten recommendations from credible people who can truly vouch for who you are and what you do.

LINKEDIN PRO TIP

When asking someone for a LinkedIn recommendation, DO NOT use the default message. Instead, customize both the subject line and the message. If you really want to be successful, you need to do a little bit of extra work.

When you ask people for a recommendation, there can be a few things that may prevent them from doing so—even for those who know and respect you and want to give you one.

For example, if your recommendation request comes when they're busy, they may think to themselves, "Oh, I'll get back to that when I have time" or "I don't really know what to write right now, so I'll just take care of this later." And they never do, because they continue to put it off or forget.

Others might find the task difficult because they have never written a recommendation before and are unsure of what it should contain or how it should be written. Again, they likely will never get around to it.

How to Get LinkedIn Recommendations

The key to getting recommendations is to make it easy for people to give them. You can do this by taking a few minutes and providing them with a sample recommendation. This will help them to know what to write.

LINKEDIN PRO TIP

I do have one caution for you.

Don't provide the same sample to everyone, because some people might actually use it verbatim. Obviously, you want to encourage them to make it their own, but some won't.

So if you send the same sample to multiple people, you might end up with five identical recommendations on your profile!

When you send a recommendation request to someone, you may want to consider offering to reciprocate. You might want to say, "I'd be happy to provide you with a recommendation also." But do that only if you feel very comfortable giving a recommendation because you know the person and his or her work.

It's also important to tell people why you're asking for their recommendation. As you customize your message, you might say something like this:

"I recently decided to spend some time improving my LinkedIn profile. I thought it would be a good idea to start getting some recommendations, and I'm hoping you can help me out. In case you were wondering what to write, I'm including a sample recommendation to give you some ideas. Also, if you're interested in receiving a LinkedIn recommendation from me, I will be more than happy to provide one for you."

In this case, it's also fine to ask them what they'd like you to say:

"Please go ahead and provide me with a sample recommendation so I can get an idea of what you'd like to see in it."

Having a complete and professional profile with recommendations will lay the foundation for your success on LinkedIn.

Before you read any further, please go ahead and complete all of the different sections of your profile that I've described in this chapter.

When you do this, you will have a killer LinkedIn profile that will place you in the top 1% to 5% of all LinkedIn members!

Chapter 4: LinkedIn Etiquette and Best Practices

Good manners are just a way of showing other people that we have respect for them.
~Bill Kelly

Each day, I see people make mistakes on LinkedIn that not only wastes their time but damages their credibility. To ensure this doesn't happen to you, it is essential that you understand and carefully utilize proper LinkedIn etiquette and best practices.

While building and growing your network, you will want to send and accept invitations to connect. There is a right way and a wrong way of doing this. In this chapter, I'm going to set out twenty principles that will keep you on the right track to growing your network effectively while building relationships and enhancing your online reputation.

1. Personalize

The first and most important tip I can share with you is to personalize **each and every connection request** that you send out. People are far more likely to accept your request if you either remind them of how they know you or explain why they should connect with you. This is especially important when connecting with people you have never met as many people on LinkedIn don't appreciate random connection requests without a personal message—

and they may even report your invitation as spam.

You may not be aware of this, but if one too many people responds to your invitations by clicking **Report Spam** or **I Don't Know This Person**, you will end up having your account restricted by LinkedIn. This will mean that you'll be required to enter an email address when sending any future LinkedIn invitations, greatly reducing your ability to connect with prospects and expand your network.

LinkedIn's default connection request message says adding a personal note is optional, but if you are connecting with someone other than your best friend, then it is *not* optional. If you follow just this one tip, you will greatly increase your success on LinkedIn, simply because most people are not doing it and you will stand out. I receive hundreds of connection requests every month and less than five percent of them are personalized in any way. In fact, personalized invites are so rare that when I see one, I almost always accept it.

Later in this book, I'll go into detail and provide you with sample messages to help you do this well.

LINKEDIN PRO TIP

Beware of sending invites using apps on mobile devices as they tend to make it difficult to send anything but the standard connection request.

2. Send a Welcome Message

When someone accepts an invitation to join your network, send them a personalized Welcome Message. Just as you would welcome someone into your home, you should welcome them into your LinkedIn network. This is the crucial difference between simply adding connections to your network and building real relationships.

Many people tell me they are active on LinkedIn but they don't find that it generates leads. This is because they are too busy treating it as a numbers game. In order to create interest among your new connections, you must show interest in them. I will cover examples of how to create an effective Welcome Message later in the book.

3. No Spam!

Don't send spammy messages to your connections!

For example, I recently received a message from someone in my network asking me to export my entire connection list and share it with them! This is a ridiculous request for two reasons and I reported it as spam. The first reason is that I don't know this person, so why would I share something like my connection list with him. Second and more importantly, because I value those people on my list, why would I share *their* contact information without *their* permission?

Just remember that everything you send to your connections should be positioned for their benefit, not yours. If it's not, then it is considered spam!

LINKEDIN PRO TIP

On a related note, there are people that will export their connections and add them to their email database. This is a very *bad* practice. Just because someone has connected with you on LinkedIn does *NOT* give you permission to add them to your email database and start sending them unsolicited emails.

4. No Facebook Like Requests

One of the biggest LinkedIn etiquette mistakes is asking people to "Like" your

Facebook page. LinkedIn and Facebook are very different social networks, and many users of one never use the other. Do NOT ask a new LinkedIn connection to like your Facebook page.

If you have developed a relationship with someone and you know they use Facebook, it may be fine to connect with them personally later on, but don't randomly ask your connections to like your Facebook business page. You'll get a lot more leverage from developing and building that relationship on LinkedIn, so why turn them off with such a request.

5. Who's Viewed Your Profile

It's a great idea to regularly check who's viewed your profile but don't send out messages saying, "I see you viewed my profile." That just feels creepy! Just because someone looked at your profile doesn't mean you need to mention it.

If the person who viewed your profile is someone you want to connect with, by all means do so, but have another reason to make the request and don't mention their visit to your profile.

6. Respond Promptly

Just as with email, the promptness of your response is often just as important as the message itself. Like email, one or two days are acceptable but don't let it go beyond that before you respond to a message on LinkedIn.

7. Professional Headshot

People choose all sorts of inappropriate photographs to use in their LinkedIn profiles. Remember, LinkedIn is a professional business network and your photograph should reflect that. Don't include anyone else—or your cat—in your photograph. It should be a clean headshot of you facing the camera, preferably smiling with a nice clean background.

Unprofessional looking photographs can make you look like a spammer, damage your credibility, and prevent people from connecting with you.

8. Don't Over Post

Don't post too many status updates. Once or twice a day is fine. Make sure you are posting information your connections will find interesting or useful. Unlike Facebook or Twitter, LinkedIn is not the place to post personal trivia in your updates—remember, stick to business and don't overwhelm your connections with too many updates.

9. Privacy Settings

Privacy settings are there for your protection, but don't forget this is a social network and you want to engage with other people. With this in mind, make your contact list open to connections, make your activity feed open to everyone, and make your name and profile open to everyone.

If there are some people who you don't want to share your information with, then they shouldn't be a part of your network, and you should remove them as a connection.

LINKEDIN PRO TIP

One important setting you should change is the one that says, "Viewers of this profile also viewed".

This is the LinkedIn default, and it can easily result in your competitors showing up at the side of the screen when someone finds you—not something you want! So uncheck that box in your settings.

---

10. Protect Other People's Privacy

When you send a message to multiple people at one time, always uncheck the box that allows recipients to see one another's names and email addresses. By not doing so, not only does it make it obvious that it was not a personal message, but it is also a serious violation of privacy that most people don't appreciate.

Image 4.1: Always uncheck the "Allow recipients to see each other's names and email addresses" box when sending a message to more than one person.

11. Endorsements

Don't ask someone to endorse your skills unless they are friends, family, colleagues, a client, or someone who knows you well.

One of the best ways to get endorsements is to give them. When you endorse someone, that person receives a notification and will often reciprocate by endorsing you.

12. Recommendation Requests

Always personalize your requests for recommendations. There are default messages for many LinkedIn functions, including this one, but I never recommend you use them. Always personalize messages, including recommendation requests.

13. Don't Ask Strangers for Recommendations

Never ask people you don't know for recommendations. If they don't know you or have never experienced your services, they can't possibly give you a genuine recommendation, so don't ask.

By the same token, never give a recommendation to someone that you don't know or whose services you have never experienced. Your credibility is on the line if that person turns out to be less than professional.

14. Nurture Your Relationships

Nurture your LinkedIn relationships through regular engagement. Send messages of congratulations on a new job, a happy birthday wish, or other simple value-based messages when appropriate.

LinkedIn makes this very easy by providing you with a daily list of these connections at the top of your Contacts page as well as an update email detailing your connections' job changes and birthdays. This is described in greater detail later in the book. You can also nurture new relationships by engaging in the content your connections share by liking and commenting on their posts.

15. Ongoing Contact

Nurture your relationships on an ongoing basis by sending messages tailored to each contact's individual needs. Make an effort to reach out to your valued connections whenever it makes sense via a personal message. If you come across content that would be of interest or of value to them, send it to them in a message. You will want to take advantage of LinkedIn Notes and Tags for ongoing follow up. I'll share more about this later on in the book.

16. Provide Value

In all your relationship building and nurturing activities, you should strive to provide value to people. The idea is to eventually move the relationships off-line, and you'll do that more effectively by giving value. Later, we will work on your message scripts to make you are a champion at this.

> One of the best ways to get value from LinkedIn is to make good use of **LinkedIn Groups**, but you have to do it right. So the next two principles relate to Groups.

17. No Self-Serving Posts In Groups

As both a group owner and a member of numerous groups, I, all too often, see people post promotional information about themselves and their businesses with no thought given to adding value to the other group members. Many group owners will simply remove offenders for this. Even if you are not removed, if you do this, you will start to be seen as a spammer and other group members will ignore your posts.

So don't post self-serving content. If you want to share your own content, make sure you craft it for the specific group you are posting in and make sure your goal is to provide value first and foremost.

18. Keep It Positive - Groups

Another major faux pas is to criticize others in the group or comment negatively. I often see people in heated debates, which serve no purpose other than to turn many people off. LinkedIn groups are a great place to make new connections, but this is not the way to do it. Keep your comments positive and *never* be insulting.

19. Keep It Professional

Remember, LinkedIn is not Facebook. When I say keep it professional, I mean don't talk about anything on LinkedIn that isn't related to business. Ever! LinkedIn is a business social network and people expect things to be professional at all times.

Facebook, Twitter, and LinkedIn are all great social networks, but it's important to understand the differences. Personal trivia may be popular on the other two, but it has no place on LinkedIn.

20. Introduce People

Finally, here is a LinkedIn best practice that can create great social capital for you: introduce your connections to each other. Think of yourself as a business matchmaker. Doing this will invoke the Law of Reciprocity[15] and often people will return the favor and introduce you to some of their connections, thus expanding your network in a very personal way. This is a great opportunity to support your connections and nurture relationships.

It's essential that you expand your LinkedIn network and use it in the right way. By following these twenty best practices, you will not only appear credible and professional but also improve the effectiveness of your lead generation efforts.

---

[15] Cialdini, Robert. (1993). *Influence: The psychology of persuasion.* New York: William Morrow. *"The rules say that we should try to repay, in kind, what another person has provided us."*

Chapter 5:
The Social Selling Process: Creating a LinkedIn Lead Generation Plan

"Social media channels offer the opportunity to build relationships with a limitless amount of possibilities globally. The best part is that most of these channels are free to join or create accounts. Through these social media channels, your sales organization has the ability to access unlimited information, prospects, and alliances or channel partnerships."
~ Jonathan Catley

Now that you have created a professional looking profile and understand LinkedIn's best practices, I am going to explain the four crucial steps that make up the social selling process. These steps can be applied to any social media platform.

A lead generation plan on LinkedIn should follow these four steps:

1. Prospecting

2. Making First Contact

3. Building Relationships

4. Taking The Relationship To the Next Level

Step 1: Prospecting

You'll remember that we talked earlier in the book about creating a clear picture of your ideal clients. Understanding and using the language of your ideal client is essential for this step to be successful.

There are two ways to prospect on LinkedIn. The first is by looking for prospects and the second is by making it easier for them to find you.

By laying the foundation with a professional and keyword-optimized profile (which I showed you how to do earlier), you have already made it easier for prospects to find you.

The other method of prospecting is to actively look for your ideal clients. There are two places in LinkedIn that you can search for prospects, the first is using the Advanced Search function and the second is through LinkedIn Groups, both of which I will explain in more detail later on.

Step 2: Making First Contact

After you have located potential prospects, you will need to make first contact. This process starts with your initial connection request. You must make sure that the connection request is personalized, telling people why they should connect with you. What you put in your connection request message will largely determine your success, so I have created a whole chapter that specifically covers the different types of messages you will need to send to connections and how to write them. I have also included a number of examples as well. Be sure you complete this and the other message scripts covered later in the book.

Step 3: Building Relationships

This step consists of building relationship with your connections and is a vital piece to the social selling process. After someone accepts your connection request, you need to keep the momentum going. If someone has sent a message to you after accepting your request, keep the conversation going. If your connection did not send a message, you can send your new connection a personalized welcome or thank you message and start a conversation to learn more about him or her.

If a prospect makes first contact by sending you a connection request, you should reply by thanking the person for connecting with you. This is also a great chance to start building the relationship by offering your new contact something of value. For example, you might share a helpful checklist, article, video, case study, eBook, or other download.

Depending on your lead generation plan, you may choose to send another relationship building message or two over the next several weeks.

LINKEDIN PRO TIP

The content of these messages will depend greatly on your industry and goals, but should NOT include anything that could be perceived as sales materials or a sales pitch of any sort!

Many people make the mistake of trying to sell or pitch their product or services right away. Don't do that because it's the fastest way to kill a potential relationship.

Step 4: Taking the Relationship to the Next Level

Finally, you need to move the relationship to the next level. Essentially, you need to move the relationship off-line. No relationship with a potential prospect should be kept solely on LinkedIn or on any online platform.

If you have provided great value to your connections in order to become a credible resource and build rapport, they will actually want to take the relationship off-line—be it through a phone call, a Skype meeting, or even an in-person meeting. It is off-line where you will convert a prospect to a client.

I want to share another powerful social selling case study that demonstrates the powerful impact of social selling. Let me introduce you to Elio Gatto, a former sales account manager and current social selling consultant and trainer.

Social Selling Case Study 4 - Elio Gatto of Social Know How Inc

http://www.linkedin.com/in/eliogatto

Elio Gatto has been social selling using a variety of social media platforms since 2007 and using LinkedIn specifically since 2012. His passion for social selling on LinkedIn is clearly visible when he shares:

> *"Utilizing LinkedIn strategically to stay connected, share, and engage is as important as a sword to a warrior. Generating leads is similar to a battle, so why not be prepared with the best tools and strategy to win!"*

In fact, Elio was featured on Social Selling with the Sharks[16] in the fall of 2013 for his success using social selling on LinkedIn.

Prior to becoming a LinkedIn social seller, Elio would generate leads through traditional forms of selling such as cold calls, in person networking events, referrals, handing out business cards, and word of mouth. While he believes that many of these are still viable options, they are much more

---

[16] LinkedIn Sales Solutions YouTube Page http://youtu.be/T73Z9dL1emk

effective and successful when used in association with LinkedIn.

The Challenge

Elio began to notice that his traditional sales methods were not working as well as they once had.

He also noticed that buyers now had the resources to obtain information they need on a product or service quicker and easier than ever before because of social media and the Internet. He understood that people typically wanted to gain insight and learn more about who was contacting them prior to having a deep conversation.

Because of this, the buying and selling process had changed, and in order to succeed in this new social world, Elio knew he needed to evolve as well and become a social seller.

The Solution

Elio, a LinkedIn member since 2008, used the platform primarily as an online resume. In 2012, while he was working as an Account Manager for an IT Solutions and Services company, he determined that he was not using the site to its full potential.

His job consisted of drumming up new business. In the beginning he relied on more traditional sales strategies like cold calling. He made call after call and was not getting anywhere. So he stopped calling and thought, *"Why am I calling people when the majority of people use email or social media to stay connected, learn, and communicate?"*

He had over one thousand connections on LinkedIn at the time and a large network of people who were sharing their professional history on their profiles. He asked himself, *"Why am I falling into this traditional sales approach trap and not utilizing this powerful LinkedIn tool to network my way into connecting with my targeted audience?"* Then he started reading numerous online articles about LinkedIn and how it was evolving.

Elio realized that while sales people were not always good at marketing themselves, he needed to brand and market himself as a *knowledge expert*. By embracing technology, social media, and marketing, he understood that the best way to reach his targeted audience was to go where they were hanging out, both personally and professionally.

It was at this point that he focused his energy on generating new leads and sales using LinkedIn and social selling!

As part of his strategy, he updated his profile, added recommendations to increase his credibility, and made sure that his profile appeared clean and professional.

He then went about creating very specific messages to send to his connections.

These messages had a subject line that was only 35 characters long and a body that was 80 to 100 words long. This ensured that the messages were short enough that his connections didn't even have to scroll down on their handheld devices. The message included three bullet points that a connection's eyes would be drawn to, a call to action, and a P.S. as people are almost always drawn to read them.

He then signed up for LinkedIn's premium service called Sales Navigator[17]. This allowed him to create and send InMails[18] to his prospects.

This strategy proved effective and allowed him to start bringing in new business.

---

[17] http://business.linkedin.com/sales-solutions/prospecting-tool.html
[18] InMails are messages that you can send to people on LinkedIn that you are NOT connected to and are seven times more likely to respond to than emails

The Results

One example of a new opportunity that he was able to close involved a new business owner who he connected with on LinkedIn. Just from reading his profile, Elio was able to gain insight into how to relate and help the business owner before they even spoke. Then, when they met in person, they discussed a solution and he closed the sale which brought in $25,000 worth of new business.

Social selling has increased Elio's sales leads overall by 25 to 50% and he is now able to focus on quality vs. quantity. Using LinkedIn, he is able to connect with buyers in a way that is more personal than the phone and provides prospective clients with a chance to get to know a bit about Elio from his own profile.

His contacts now perceive him as someone who offers them value and is a knowledge expert rather than just a salesperson.

Takeaways

There are a number of concepts that Elio keeps in mind when creating his messages or reaching out to a prospective lead.

- Don't use LinkedIn messages to sell but rather to warmly lead prospective clients into setting up a meeting. Then sell in person!

- Have a strong and clean LinkedIn profile that shows who you are and how you can help prospective clients. Not just what you offer!

- Make sure that your messages are mobile and app friendly. Every connection request, message, or InMail should fit perfectly on a smartphone screen to minimize scrolling. The message should also include bullets points that relate to your audience.

- Track which messages get the best response and regularly tweak and improve them as necessary.

• Know who you want to connect with and spend time where they hang out, whether online or in person. Put yourself in the customers' shoes and consider how they will respond to your approach and messaging. Ask yourself, "Would I really take a few seconds to read past the intro?"

In his own words, Elio shares,

"Think of your LinkedIn profile as your professional online WORLD presence. How you present yourself on LinkedIn is how you are typically perceived professionally online by others. For example, would you go to a business meeting wearing your track pants and a ripped t-shirt? I highly doubt you would, unless you are there to prove some sort of point. Therefore, why would you leave your LinkedIn profile incomplete and put no effort into utilizing it. I'd say that being on LinkedIn without engagement or knowledge sharing is worse than not being on LinkedIn at all."

Let's move on to Part II where I will help you to build your lead generation plan. I will provide a number of examples and exercises to help you create each step of your daily checklist and message scripts.

Part II

Creating Your Social Selling Campaign

Chapter 6: LinkedIn Lead Generation Plan

"Social is not a place for a hard sell—it's a place to build trust and credibility. Work the intelligence into your formal sales process and messaging while staying top of mind by continuing to interact on a personal level over social media."
~Julio Viskovich

As part of your social selling efforts, you will need to create a lead generation plan on LinkedIn. This plan will include specific actions that you will need to do daily and weekly to effectively generate new leads and contacts.

It doesn't matter if you spend fifteen minutes a day or one hour a day. What does matter is that you are consistent.

Before I cover each of the tasks you will need to include in your plan, I first want to cover three vital concepts you will need to be familiar with.

1. Grow Your Network
2. Monitor and Engage Your Network
3. Utilize LinkedIn Groups

Grow Your Network

People can only find you if you're in their 1st, 2nd or 3rd degree networks[19]

---

[19] Your 1st degree network is anyone you are directly connected to, your 2nd degree network includes the contacts of your 1st degree contacts, and your 3rd degree network includes the contacts of your 2nd degree network.

or if you're a member of the same group. So, it's really important to grow your network. Remember, this isn't Facebook. You don't need to guard and protect your network. Obviously, you won't connect with anyone who looks suspicious or looks like a potential spammer, just as there may also be some people that you do not want to be connected to. There could be any number of reasons why you won't want to accept connection requests from certain people, but for the most part, it's good to accept invitations to connect. It's a win-win situation because every single person you connect with expands your network further.

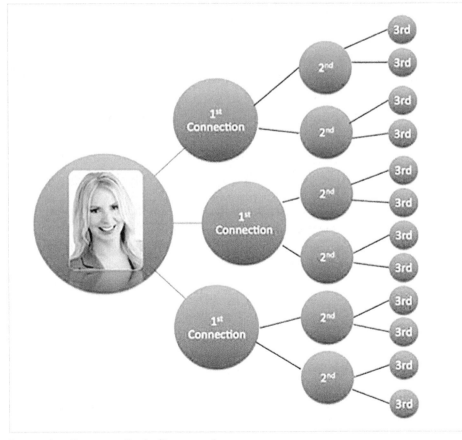

Image 6.1: Grow your LinkedIn network.

Growing your network is essential to increasing your chances of being found when someone does a LinkedIn search for what you offer. **If you are not in their network, you won't show up.** This is also very important as you start using LinkedIn to reach out to potential prospects since you are limited to finding people that are within your network.

Monitor & Engage Your Network

Once you have a network of people built up, you need to monitor your network to see what's going on with your connections and to interact and engage with them on a regular basis. You might, for example, comment on their status updates, "like" their comments, congratulate them on changes that have happened, or even send random value-based messages.

If you come across something that you think would be a good fit for some of the people in your network—perhaps an article, a video, or a relevant stat—send it to them. Let them know that you've just come across something you think would be of value to them.

Make introductions when appropriate. Help your connections meet other people that might have some value for them, such as a supplier, vendor, or potential prospect. The best part about this is that when you start doing this for other people, many will do it for you too. Reciprocity will happen.

You might also ask your connections for introductions. If there's somebody you want to meet, and you know someone who they're connected to, ask that person for an introduction.

> ## LINKEDIN PRO TIP
>
> When asking one of your connections to make an introduction to someone in their network, make sure they actually know that person. If they do, you can ask them for a warm introduction. If your connection doesn't actually know the person you want to connect with, send the person a personalized connection request stating why you would like to connect.

Provide endorsements and recommendations, when appropriate, for your connections. By doing this, you'll also invoke the Law of Reciprocity and many will reciprocate by endorsing or recommending you. (Remember, you should never do this for somebody unless you can truly vouch for their credibility and their expertise.)

Utilize LinkedIn Groups

LinkedIn allows you to join up to fifty groups. One of the keys to expanding your network is to join as many relevant groups as possible.

One of the biggest mistakes people make is to only join their industry specific groups. To effectively use LinkedIn Groups, you want to join groups that are **specific to your target clients**.

Begin by looking at the groups you're already part of, decide if they're right for you, and remove the ones that are not. Next, start searching for other groups you might want to join.

If your business focuses on your local area, then you will want to search out and join all relevant local groups. If, for example, you lived in Vancouver, you would type *Vancouver* into the search box in Groups and see what groups come up. Review these groups and determine which ones might be a good fit for you.

When reviewing groups, there are some specific things you should pay attention to. First, how many members are in the group? The more members a group has, the more your network expands. Be aware though that it isn't just a numbers game. There might be a group with only a few hundred members, but it may be a very targeted niche group filled with your ideal clients. In this case, it might make sense for you to join.

Next, how many discussions have happened in the group this month? This will tell you how active the group is. If you see a group that has no activity, you might not want to join that group. In some cases, it might still make sense for you if your only purpose is to review the members and be able to reach out and connect with them.

LINKEDIN PRO TIP

When you're a member of a group, you can send messages to the other members for free, rather than having to send an InMail.

If you only have a 2nd or 3rd level connection with someone but are not in a group with them, you can only message them with an InMail, which is a paid service on LinkedIn. But if both of you are members of the same group, you can message them through the group for free. This is a great connection tool and a good reason to belong to fifty groups—the maximum LinkedIn allows.

A good way to use this function to your advantage is to go to a specific group and look at its members. You can either scroll through to find people of interest to you, or if you are looking for a specific member, you can type in the person's name. When you find someone you want to reach out to, you can do it via message even though you may only be 2nd or 3rd level connections.

Most of the groups you join should be groups that attract your target market. As I mentioned earlier, many people make the mistake of joining only their own industry-related groups (e.g., financial advisors join financial advisor groups). But the people in those groups are people in your industry and, of course, your competitors! That's not what you want—you want to join groups where you target market is.

You may want to join some industry groups because this will help you see what your peers are doing, stay up to date on industry trends, and even watch your competitors. If you decide to do this, limit it to three to five groups in this category.

You may also want to join a few groups (up to five) relating to a special interest you have. For example, if you're interested in learning more about social media or LinkedIn, you could join a few social media groups that provide good content.

But the vast majority of your groups [40+] should be specific to your target market because this will expand your ability to reach out and connect with those people through connection requests and allow you to take advantage of the free messaging option.

Remember, if someone is searching for what you offer, you'll only show up if you are a 1st, 2nd or 3rd degree connection—or if you are a member of the same group. This gives you an opportunity to connect with people who are actually looking for what you have to offer. Are you beginning to see the value of LinkedIn Groups when you use them correctly?

Chapter 7:
The Essentials of Your
Action Plan

"A goal without a plan is just a wish."
~ Antoine de Saint-Exupéry

In this chapter, I'm going to cover, in great detail, the essential actions you will need to include as part of your lead generation plan. You will then take each of these activities and use them to create your own daily and weekly checklists in the next chapter.

Now let's dive into the specific actions you will want to perform on a daily and weekly basis as part of your lead generation plan on LinkedIn.

Post Your Status Updates

Posting daily status updates should be the first thing on your LinkedIn checklist. You should update your status once a day. People in your network will see in their news feed when you post an update. This will help to keep you top of mind and help position you as a knowledge expert. Make sure you are sharing valuable content that's of specific interest and value to your ideal prospects.

If you have your own blog, post a LinkedIn update every time you post to your blog. You can also post updates when you find interesting content from other people.

> ## LINKEDIN PRO TIP
>
> If you have social sharing buttons on your blog, which I recommend, you can share your posts on LinkedIn directly from the blog itself.

Whether you post your own or other people's content, it's important to add your own comment. A useful trick is to make the comment in the form of a question which is often more likely to start a conversation.

Let's say, for example, I am sharing an article on social selling called *5 Steps to Leverage LinkedIn for More Sales*. I may add a question like, "Have you been successful at getting new leads & clients from LinkedIn?"

Try not to post updates more than twice a day as this can be irritating and seen as spammy by your connections.

Reply to and Welcome New Connections

If you have created a profile that is well optimized for your keywords and speaks to your ideal clients, then you will start to receive more frequent connection requests from others. One of the first things you want to do at the beginning of your time each day on LinkedIn is to accept incoming connection requests. After you accept a connection request, you should send a welcome message to your new connection.

One of the message scripts you will be creating is your *Welcome / Thank You Message*. You will use this script to reply to and welcome all your new connections.

You can have multiple welcome messages if you have multiple target markets. You should further personalize the message whenever possible and tweak it as necessary. It is a good idea to keep your message scripts all on one page and open on your computer while you are accepting new connections.

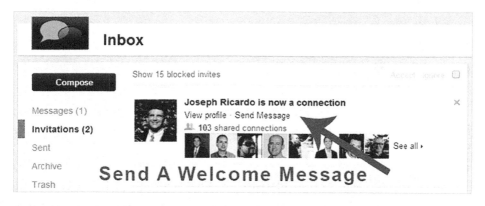

Image 7.1: Send a welcome message after accepting a connection request.

It is then as simple as scrolling down to the correct welcome script, copying and pasting it into your message, and then personalizing it. You can quickly and easily begin to establish relationships with your new connections.

Make sure your message is relevant to the person you are sending it to. For example, if your script mentions sales managers and this is a salesperson and not a manager, you'll need to tweak the message to fit the intended recipient. I like to go further and include the person's name in the subject line, which clearly shows that the message is personal and not an identical message sent out to fifty people.

When accepting a connection request that has been personalized, it is important to ensure that you modify your message to address each of the points that are a part of the message to you. Sending an unmodified message will give the impression that the person is not worth your time to reply to personally and will hurt the relationship you are trying to build before it even begins.

So every time you click Accept, make sure you send your welcome message. You will also want to send a message to every person who accepts a connection request you send. After they accept your request, send them your *Welcome /*

Thank You Message.

Respond to Messages

Next, check all your messages and respond. As I mentioned earlier in the best practices chapter, it is important to make sure that you reply in a timely manner.

LinkedIn, like every other platform online, is going to bring you some spam. When you get a spam message, you can choose to do one of two things. You can either delete the message or you can hit Report Spam.

In many cases, the person doesn't know they are doing anything wrong, in which case it is best to just delete the message. However, in order to ensure that LinkedIn will continue to be useful to everyone, it is the responsibility of each person to learn and use the best practices of the platform.

Send Connection Requests

Next, send connection requests to people you know or just met using the message script you wrote for that purpose. For example, if you just attended an event and you met some people you want to stay in contact with, send them a connection request right away, mentioning that you just met them at the event. Once they've connected with you, then you can start the follow-up process to build the relationship.

Finding New Connections

I suggest you set a target for the number of new prospects you will reach out to every day—five or ten would be ideal. There are a number of places where you can search for prospects to connect with, such as LinkedIn's Advanced Search and LinkedIn Groups.

Using Advanced Search

LinkedIn's Advanced Search tool is great for finding potential prospects to connect with.

The Advanced Search uses what is known as a Boolean search[20], and this gives you a number of ways to filter your search so that you find exactly what you are looking for. You do this by specifically eliminating elements you don't want. Here is a summary of how to use Boolean search parameters in LinkedIn's Advanced Search.

Using Boolean Search Parameters in LinkedIn's Advanced Search

Quotes

If you would like to search for an exact phrase, you can enclose the phrase in quotation marks. You can use these in addition to other modifiers.

Examples:

"product manager"

"account representative"

"executive assistant"

Parenthetical

If you would like to do a complex search, you can combine terms and modifiers. For instance, the first example will find both software engineers and software architects.

---

[20] Boolean searches allow you to combine words and phrases using the words AND, OR, NOT and NEAR (otherwise known as Boolean operators) to limit, widen, or define your search. About.com (http://websearch.about.com/od/2/g/boolean.htm)

Examples:

software AND (engineer or architect)

(instructional designer OR instructional design) e-learning

(human resources) AND "customer service"

AND

If you would like to search for profiles which include two terms, you can separate those terms with the upper-case word **AND**. However, you don't have to use AND—if you enter two terms, the search program will assume that there is an AND between them.

Examples:

software AND engineer

software+engineer [You can also add a plus + in between the words with no space]

"customer service" AND hospitality

"instructional design" AND "e-learning"

software engineer

OR

If you would like to broaden your search to find profiles which include one or more terms, you can separate those terms with the upper-case word **OR**.

Examples:

"Pitney Bowes" OR "Hewlett-Packard"

Helpdesk OR "Help Desk" OR "Technical Support"

"Vice President" OR VP OR "V.P." OR SVP OR EVP

J2EE OR "Java Enterprise Edition" OR JEE OR JEE5

"account executive" OR "account exec" OR "account manager" OR "sales executive" OR "sales manager" OR "sales representative"

NOT

If you would like to do a search but exclude a particular term, type that term with an upper-case **NOT** immediately before it. Your search results will exclude any profile containing that term.

Examples:

NOT director

(Google OR Salesforce) NOT LinkedIn

director NOT executive NOT VP NOT "Vice President"

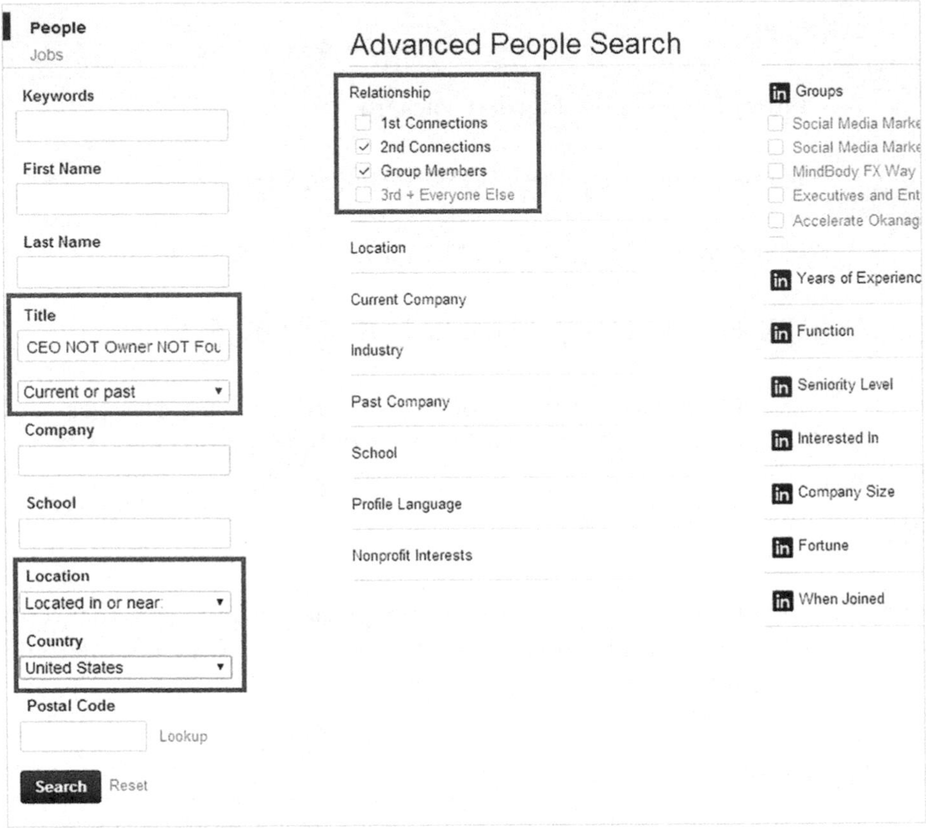

Image 7.2: Use a Boolean Search to narrow your search results.

So, for example, if I was looking for a CEO of a large company, not a business owner, founder, or consultant, I would use the Boolean tools in the Advanced Search function. Under Title, I can specify the exact search requirements I have. The search would look like this.

CEO NOT Owner NOT Founder NOT Consultant

If I want results from the U.S. instead of Canada, I can change that parameter in my Advanced Search. Now, this doesn't mean that all the people who come up will always be perfectly targeted, but it will definitely narrow your search down. You can continue narrowing your search down by geography, by company, and by other filters to find exactly what you want.

You should also remove 1st degree connections from your search parameters because they are already part of your network. You are looking for 2nd degree connections and group members you can reach out to and connect with. While using a Boolean search will lower the number of results you get, it will also make them much more tightly focused.

You can also use Advanced Search with Groups. Let's say, for example, you want to use your ability to send group members a message to reach and connect with somebody. Using the parameters in an Advanced Search, simply uncheck everything except Group Members. Alternatively, you can look for people within specific groups.

Let's say, for example, I wanted to connect with consultants in the Calgary Business Networking group. I simply select that group, add in the keyword *consultant,* and hit search. This will bring up only people with the word Consultant in their profile within that Calgary group and nobody else. I urge you to play with this and try a variety of different parameters.

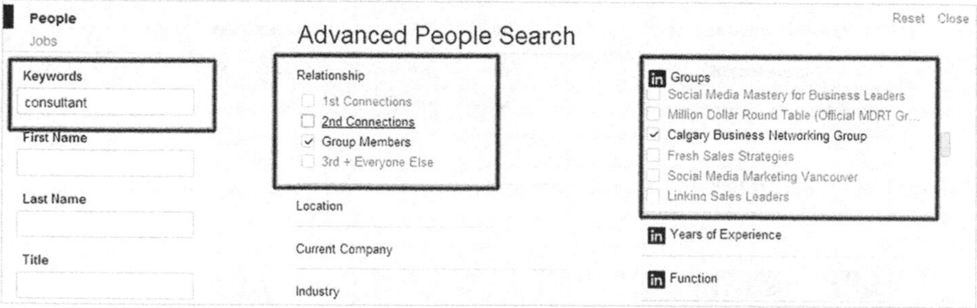

Image 7.3: Use a Boolean Search to find prospects from a specific group.

> ## LINKEDIN PRO TIP
>
> If you have a paid account, you can also look at company size. You can look for Fortune 1000, Fortune 500, Fortune 100 or Fortune 50 companies.
>
> The extra Advanced Search options are one of the main differences between the free and paid accounts on LinkedIn.

Saved Searches

If you find a particular search that is producing great results, you can save that search. This is a really powerful tool because the search program keeps track of when people who match your saved criteria join LinkedIn or update their profiles. You can come back to these search results at any time and check for new potential clients. You can then go through each of these new profiles and reach out to connect with any potential prospects.

Saved Searches

Type	Title	New	Alert	Created		
People	**CEO Fortune 1000 US**	33	Weekly	Jul 26, 2013	✎	✕
People	**Manager Fortune 1000 US**	62	Weekly	Jul 26, 2013	✎	✕
People	**VP Fortune 1000 US**	62	Weekly	Jul 26, 2013	✎	✕
People	**VP of Sales United States VP**	394	Monthly	Apr 11, 2013	✎	✕

Image 7.4: Save searches that are producing great results.

Basically, this is LinkedIn sending targeted prospects to your mailbox! Furthermore, LinkedIn will send you an email once a week or once a month with any new profiles that match your Saved Search parameters. With a free account you can set up three saved search results.

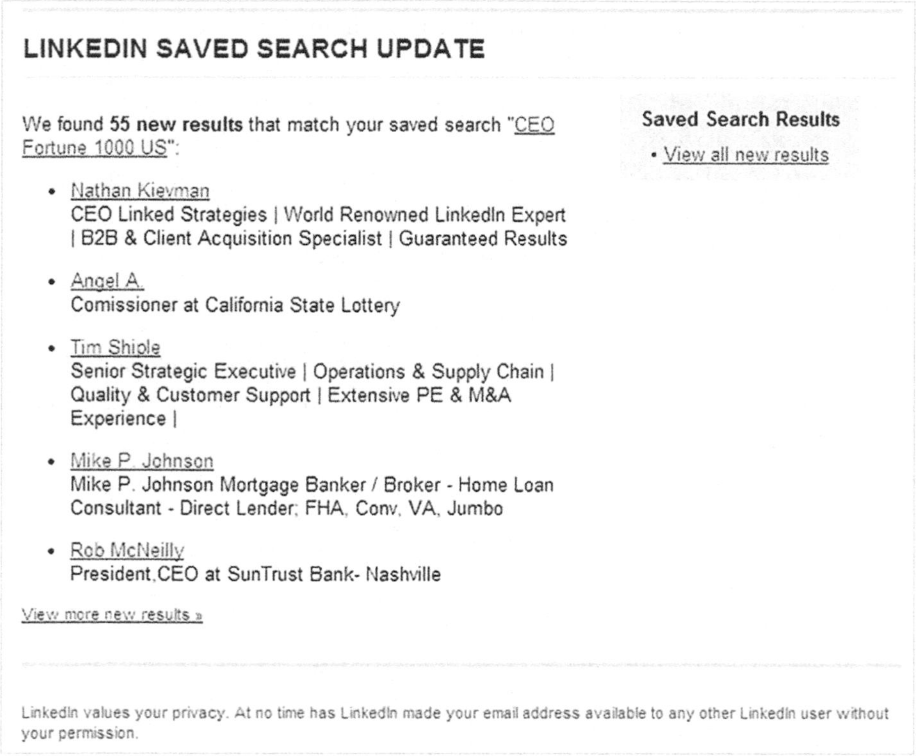

LINKEDIN SAVED SEARCH UPDATE

We found **55 new results** that match your saved search "CEO Fortune 1000 US":

Saved Search Results
- View all new results

- Nathan Kievman
  CEO Linked Strategies | World Renowned LinkedIn Expert | B2B & Client Acquisition Specialist | Guaranteed Results

- Angel A.
  Comissioner at California State Lottery

- Tim Shiple
  Senior Strategic Executive | Operations & Supply Chain | Quality & Customer Support | Extensive PE & M&A Experience |

- Mike P. Johnson
  Mike P. Johnson Mortgage Banker / Broker - Home Loan Consultant - Direct Lender; FHA, Conv, VA, Jumbo

- Rob McNeilly
  President,CEO at SunTrust Bank- Nashville

View more new results »

LinkedIn values your privacy. At no time has LinkedIn made your email address available to any other LinkedIn user without your permission.

Image 7.5: You will receive an email with a list of potential prospects from your Saved searches.

Check Out Who's Viewed Your Profile

When people view your profile, it presents an opportunity to connect with them. As I mentioned in the etiquette section, I do not advise starting your connection request by saying, "I saw you viewed my profile." However, you can certainly reach out to those people by using one of your personalized connection request messages and offering to be a resource for them.

If they're looking at your profile, it might be that they want some information about you, so why not offer it to them?

As an example, one of my own message scripts for this situation says, "*I'd love to connect with you here on LinkedIn. As your sales team explores using social media, feel free to use me as a resource for social selling. I have tons of free content from blog posts and articles and videos.*" With this, I am starting to build a relationship with that person by offering free and valuable content right from the start.

With a free account, you'll only see the last five people who viewed your profile, but if you have a paid account, you'll see every single person who's viewed your profile.

When you are just getting started with LinkedIn and until you have a really big network, you might find that there are five or fewer people viewing your profile a day, but as you improve your profile and build your network, that number could dramatically increase. At that point, you might consider upgrading to a premium account so that you can see everybody who has viewed your profile or to filter these members using the premium advanced search functions. I will explain these in a later chapter.

Either way, it's a good opportunity to see if there are people you want to connect with who have already shown some interest in your profile.

Warm Introductions

You should also look for warm introductions. Whenever possible, review your 1st degree connections and see who they're connected with. Look for opportunities for an introduction and leverage your 1st degree connection as a conversation starter. This could take the form of asking your connection the question, "I see we're both connected to this person. Do you know them personally, or are you just connected on LinkedIn?" If they say they do know them personally, then you can ask for a warm introduction.

Relationship-Building Messages

Your relationship-building messages are designed to build rapport with your new connections. Once you've connected with someone, follow up with your welcome message. Then set a reminder to start your relationship-building messages the following week. You can set these reminders by using the **Reminder** feature located in the **Relationship** tab on the profile page of your connection. I will go into more detail on the Relationship tab later.

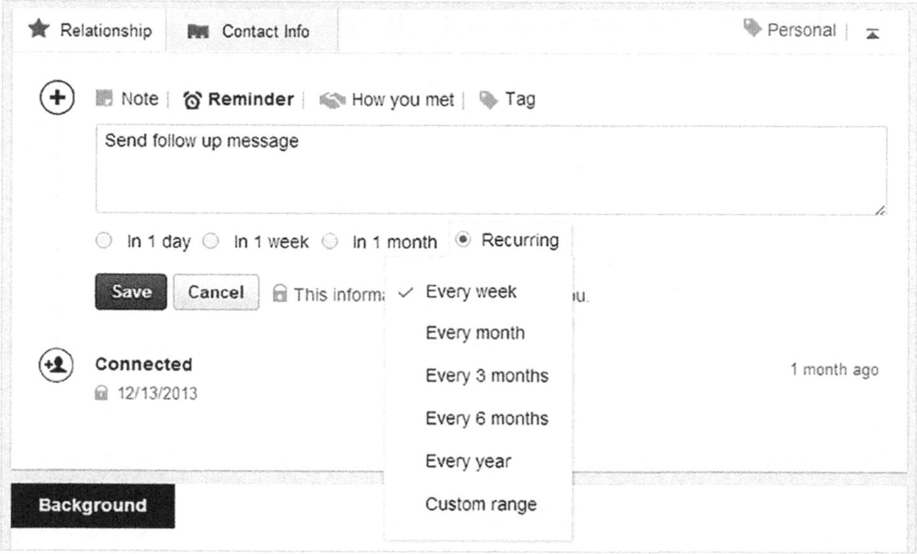

Image 7.6: Set a Reminder to follow up in the Relationship tab.

LINKEDIN PRO TIP

You can set reminders to occur in a day, a week, or a month as well as recurring reminders.

If a dialogue begins between you and another person before you have a chance to send your next follow up message, you'll have to tweak your pre-written message as appropriate. Fortunately, LinkedIn makes it easy to keep track of your conversations with your connections in the Relationship tab. In this tab, you will find all the messages and conversations you've had with a contact. Based on what you find, you can set a reminder for when you want to send them a message, and you can double check that you haven't had any other contact with them in the meantime.

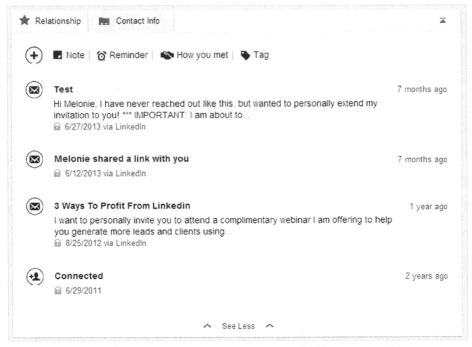

Image 7.7: See your history of contact with a prospect in the Relationship Tab.

Manage Your Relationship With Your Connections

I mentioned several of the helpful capabilities that are a part of the Relationship tab. This tab feature is an amazing organizational tool that LinkedIn offers to both free and paid members.

One of the most helpful features of the tab is the ability to access your **Tags**. Every single time you connect with a person, you should tag them and put them in a specific tag group, based on who they are. For example, are they a prospect, a strategic alliance, or an existing client?

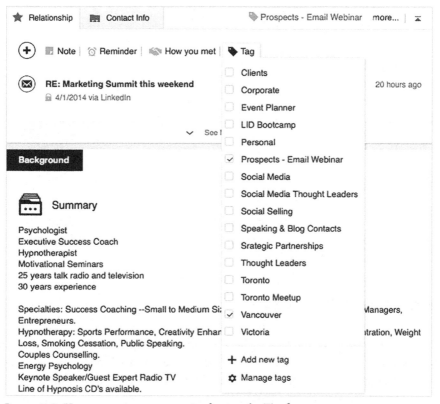

Image 7.8: Keep your contacts organized using the Tag feature.

Once you have tagged your connections into a specific group, you can add notes or set up reminders for follow-up as I mentioned previously. It is also useful to include how you met so that you can use that information in future interactions with them.

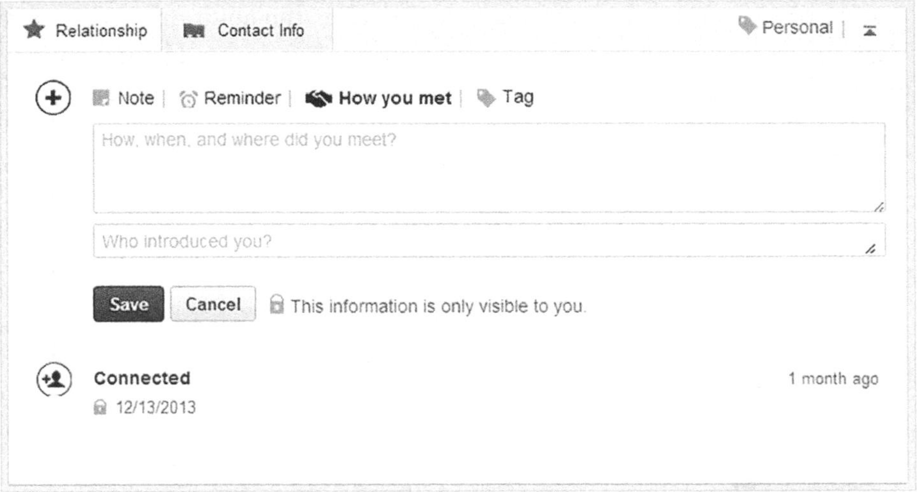

Image 7.9: Keep track of how you met a connection.

All of this information is private, so you don't have to worry about anybody seeing what you've written. This will allow you to stay focused on achieving your goal for each relationship.

Review Your Notifications

There's a little flag at the top right side of the navigation bar that contains your Notifications. Every day you should review your Notifications to look for engagement opportunities. This will show you all the people who have engaged with your content, have endorsed you, have *liked* your updates, or have taken any other action that involves you on LinkedIn. You can then look for an opportunity to connect with them or have a conversation with them.

The notifications will show you if someone has shared your content. You can also check to see if people that aren't currently connected to you are engaging with your content. This is a great opportunity to reach out and connect with them because they already know you through your content.

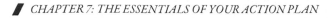

Image 7.10: Check your Notifications for opportunities to engage or connect with people.

When contacting them, you might say something like, *"I noticed your comment on my article from Social Media Examiner that Richard posted"*. This is a great opportunity to start a conversation with somebody new.

Weekly Outreach To Hot Prospects

Each week, try to reach out and share content with some of your hottest prospects.

It is a good idea to create two tag folders for your prospects: one for regular prospects and one for hot prospects. Hot prospects are the people you really want to stay in touch with, monitor, and continue to follow up with. After you've taken them through the relationship-building messages, stay in contact with them by setting up a weekly or monthly reminder.

You can become a resource for these hot prospects by sending them insightful and interesting content. If you find an article or something that's of value to them, send it.

LINKEDIN PRO TIP

If you find an article on a website that has a LinkedIn share button, use this to send it to individual connections rather than sharing the article as a status update.

You do this by simply typing in their name or email address in the dialog box that pops up when you use the share button. As I've mentioned before, always customize and personalize any communications that you send to your connections.

For example you might write,

Hi Judy,

I thought you may find this article interesting called 19 Steps To Social Selling On LinkedIn[21].

LinkedIn has been shown to be 277% more effective for lead generation than Facebook or Twitter.

And did you know that 72.6% of salespeople who use social media outperform their colleagues who aren't using it.

Let me know if you have any questions about social selling best practices, I'd be happy to answer them.

Melonie

---

[21] http://topdogsocialmedia.com/19-steps-to-social-selling-on-linkedin/

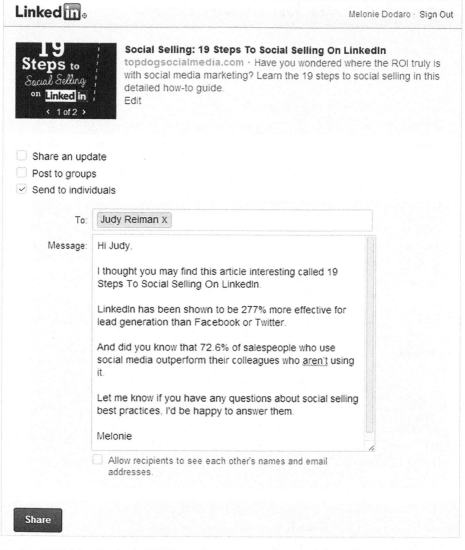

Image 7.11: Use the LinkedIn Share button to send an article or blog post to your prospects, hot prospects, and clients.

Manage And Review Your LinkedIn Contacts

Go to your different tagged groups on a regular basis and take a look at what's happening with your connections.

You can access your tagged groups by going to your Contacts page. Hover over the Network tab in the main navigation bar at the top of the page and click on Contacts. From here, you will be able to select any of your tagged groups under the *Filter by* option.

Image 7.12: Access your Tags under the Filter by option on the Contacts page.

If you have all your contacts organized and tagged, keeping track of who you connect or engage with becomes easy to manage. Review your tagged folders often to see if there's any particular person you want to follow up or engage with.

At the top of the Contacts page you will also find Notification boxes that highlight your contacts celebrating special events such as job changes, anniversaries, and birthdays. You can click on these boxes to send a special message to your contacts, helping you to stay top of mind.

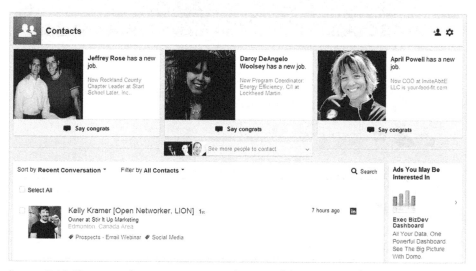

Image 7.13: Engage with your connections that are celebrating special occasions, shown in Notification Boxes at the top of the Contacts page.

LinkedIn also provides you with a daily email that notifies you of these same important events for your connections. This is a great opportunity for you to reach out and start a conversation with any of your contacts. If you see, for example, that one of your contacts has a new job, you can send a message congratulating them on that. Again, don't use the LinkedIn default messages here, but personalize what you say.

Review Your Home Page News Feed

Use the news feed on the LinkedIn home page to review content and discussions posted by your contacts that you might want to engage with.

Prepare for your day and stay in touch.   See More

Job Changes

Gustavo Loureiro has a new job.
Now Co-Founder and Visiting Lecturer at Digital Media Academy of Canada.
✉ Say congrats

Haris Beha has a new job.
Now Process Improvement Analyst at AFS Technologies, Inc..
✉ Say congrats

Mark Kendrick has a new job.
Now Manager at Nicola Browne, New Zealand Womens Cricket Player.
✉ Say congrats

Birthdays

Dragiya Stoychev's birthday is today.
Area Delivery Manager at Ericsson.
✉ Say happy birthday

Robert Scarr (LION)'s birthday is today.
Agent and Authorized Affiliate at Zane Benefits.
✉ Say happy birthday

Tabatha Bourguignon's birthday is today.
Communications & Social Media Manager at Hotspex.
✉ Say happy birthday

Image 7.14: LinkedIn will notify you by email of your contacts that are celebrating special occasions.

You can filter your news feed in a number of ways, such as only seeing when your connections have recently connected with another person. When you see that your connections have new connections, this is a great opportunity for you to make contact with new people. Pay attention to who your contacts are connecting with, especially if they are competitors. Wouldn't it be useful to see who your competitors are connecting with? You can do that here.

You can also filter by profiles and look for any changes or updates. People might have a new job, are following new people, or have updated certain parts of their profile, such as adding a new photo. Once again, this is another opportunity to reach out to your contacts. In addition, knowing of these changes allows you to take them into account when thinking of how you can provide value to them.

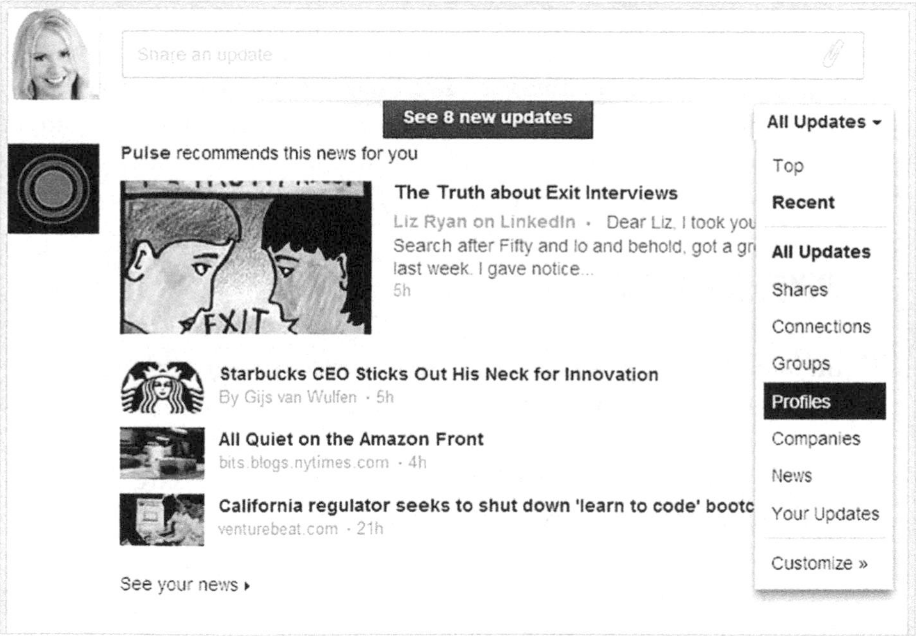

Image 7.15: Filter the content of the news feed on your Homepage.

You can also use the filters to check if there are people following new companies. See who's sharing content and engage with that person by liking or commenting on the content they shared. Play with these options to see how they can help you connect with people and start conversations.

Participating In LinkedIn Groups

It is a good idea to participate in and post a new piece of content to LinkedIn Groups once a week. This involves finding great content to share and taking the time to read content or comments posted by others and replying to these comments.

Finding And Sharing Great Content

There are many sources where you can find good articles to share as an update. One of these sources is LinkedIn's very own Pulse[22] which is particularly useful because LinkedIn knows what will be of interest to you based on the content you have in your profile. On your Home Feed, click on Pulse, and you'll see all the different articles that LinkedIn thinks you might be interested in.

LINKEDIN PRO TIP

If you find something to share, you can either click to go right to it, or you can choose to comment on it, like it, or share it.

Personally, I like to read an article before I share it to make sure that it is high quality content that is relevant to my audience.

If you're using Twitter[23], Twitter Lists[24] can be useful to find content that you want to share. Let's say for example, you want to share business-related

---

[22] http://www.linkedin.com/company/pulse-news
[23] www.twitter.com
[24] "A list is a curated group of Twitter users. You can create your own lists or subscribe to lists created by others." ~Twitter Help
(https://support.twitter.com/articles/76460-using-twitter-lists)

articles. You might create a Twitter List with great content sources such as Inc. Magazine[25], Entrepreneur Magazine[26], Forbes Magazine[27] and various other industry influencers. Your sources can be magazines, organizations, or individuals as long as they consistently post great content. Then, you can easily go to that Twitter List at any time and find content to share with your connections on LinkedIn.

Another great source is Alltop[28] which is an article site with a large variety of different categories and topics. Feedly[29] is an RSS[30] feed where you can set up specific categories of content you want to review from your favorite blogs and magazines.

Not every article you share on LinkedIn has to be one of your own. I like to share my own content in LinkedIn Groups because it not only adds value for readers, but it also leads to a lot of traffic to my website.

Posting To LinkedIn Groups

A good way to start a conversation in a LinkedIn Group is to ask a question.

For example, if I write an article on Prospecting on LinkedIn, I would post it in LinkedIn Groups with a question like, *"Have you been successful at generating new leads and clients from LinkedIn?"*

Post the question as the actual title because that is the first thing group members will see. You should also add a description with a call to action. If you'd like to stimulate a conversation here, ask them to share their thoughts in the comments below.

---

[25] @Inc (www.inc.com)
[26] @EntMagazine (www.entrepreneur.com)
[27] @Forbes (www.forbes.com)
[28] http://user-interface.alltop.com
[29] www.feedly.com
[30] "Really Simple Syndication, uses a family of standard web feed formats to publish frequently updated information: blog entries, news headlines, audio and video." Wikipedia (http://en.wikipedia.org/wiki/RSS)

If your post is relevant to several Groups, post it to all of them. However, if you send it to fifty groups at once, it will flood the news feed, which is something you do not want to do. I use a tool called Oktopost[31], which enables sharing to Groups in stages. This means that rather than sharing with fifty Groups at once, you can schedule it to post, for example, to only five Groups at a time over two or three days.

Engage In LinkedIn Groups

You should also review the news feed of the groups you are a member of and look for opportunities to engage and add value to the discussions. Doing so will increase your visibility and also attract potential prospects if you are providing educational and valuable comments.

You can also use the search tool to look for keywords that are of interest to you and your prospects or clients. This will bring up any conversations that are going on in the group around this topic. Again, this is a chance to contribute to the discussion and help build your reputation as an authority on your topic.

By posting great content and participating in a helpful way in discussions, you will also raise your Contributor standing in groups. If you reach **Top Contributor** ranking, your profile will be visible to all members and you will be seen as an expert in the group. As a **Top Contributor**, you will appear in the top right hand corner on the group's homepage.

Review Your Groups

Sometimes you will join groups where there's been little to no activity or the group moderator prevents your content from being shared because they don't allow posts with links.

---

[31] www.oktopost.com

Top Contributors in this Group

Melonie Dodaro

The media calls me Canada's #1 LinkedIn Expert ◆
Speaker: LinkedIn, Social Media, Social Selling,
Influence Marketing

See all members ›

Your group contribution level

Congrats! Regularly add great discussions and
comments to stay a Top Contributor.

Top Contributor

Image 7.16: Get great exposure in groups as an authority or expert by reaching the Top Contributor status.

Such a group will become less and less valuable to you. When there is no value left in being a member of a group you should leave that group and find a more valuable one to replace it with.

Give and Request Recommendations

I suggest you provide a recommendation to someone in your network approximately once a month. If there's somebody in your network that you feel comfortable recommending, whose credibility and expertise you can vouch for, then go ahead and write them a recommendation. When that person accepts your recommendation on their profile, LinkedIn actually prompts them to return the favor and recommend you.

Not everybody will do so, and in fact not everybody should. For example, many people recommend me because they've attended my webinars, seminars, or my online courses, but I don't know them personally. So if they provide me with a recommendation, I can't return the favor because I don't know them or their work.

Another benefit is that when you recommend people, your profile is clickable from their profile. To see what I mean by this, scroll down to the Experience section in your profile and you will see all the people who have sent you recommendations. You'll notice that their names are all clickable links. This will often result in people clicking on your profile to learn more about you.

You should also reach out and ask people for recommendations once in a while, and I strongly suggest you follow the formula I shared with you earlier in the book to do this successfully.

Image 7.17: The name of each Recommendation is a clickable link.

Endorse Other's Skills

Next, you want to endorse people in your network. This is the most popular feature of LinkedIn because it's so simple. You just click the little plus sign beside each Skill listed that you want to endorse someone for.

Unfortunately, too many people are endorsing random people they don't know, which can undermine the value of Skills. There is, however, a level of social proof here whether people realize it or not. When you see a profile of a person that has lots of endorsements with all those pictures next to them, this provides a level of social proof.

What is even more important is that those endorsements actually affect LinkedIn's algorithm and help you move higher up in the search results for those specific skills (keywords). For example, if you get a hundred endorsements for a specific keyword and somebody else has only ten endorsements for the same keyword, you could potentially show up higher in the search results.

So reach out and endorse people you know in your network on a regular basis. They will then receive a notification that you've endorsed them, and this will often result in starting a conversation and them reciprocating and endorsing some of your skills.

Send Mass Messages

While I have spoken frequently on personalization throughout this book, there may be times when it will make sense to send out mass group messages. If you want to take advantage of this feature, LinkedIn permits you to send messages to up to fifty people at one time.

Let's say, for example, you are offering a free webinar or doing an expert interview. If you wanted to let a large number of your LinkedIn contacts know about this, you can do that by sending a mass message. I use this feature when I launch new webinars, and I want to invite all my contacts in certain tags to attend.

If you have a tagged group in your network with less than fifty people in it, you can select the entire group you want to send the message to and then write a customized message to go to them. Make sure that you **uncheck** the box that allows recipients to see the names of everyone the message was sent to.

Sending a mass message to a tagged group with more than fifty people in it is a more involved process. You will need to check fifty people at a time to send the message to and then repeat the process of selecting and sending to fifty people until you have sent it to everyone in the list. This is time consuming, but valuable. This is another reason why tagging your connections is so important.

The first time I did this for a LinkedIn webinar, I doubled my email list in less than one week. Now, each of those connections is also a part of my email list and receives my weekly newsletters, allowing me to stay top of mind. They also get notifications via email of new products and courses I'm launching, which has resulted in substantial additional revenue in my business.

LINKEDIN PRO TIP

If you are not currently growing an email list and staying in touch with your connections, this is something I highly recommend to complement your LinkedIn lead generation efforts.

Chapter 8: Creating Your Action Plan

"Good checklists, on the other hand are precise. They are efficient, to the point, and easy to use even in the most difficult situations. They do not try to spell out everything—a checklist cannot fly a plane. Instead, they provide reminders of only the most critical and important steps—the ones that even the highly skilled professional using them could miss. Good checklists are, above all, practical."
~ Atul Gawande, The Checklist Manifesto: How to Get Things Right

Now that I have laid out the different tasks that will make up your lead generation campaign, it is time to put the pieces together to create your action plan or checklist.

First, you need to determine how many people you want to reach out and connect with each day. Keep in mind that not all the activities I've described need to be done daily. Some of them are only done once a week, some twice a week. Some are monthly or even less. Sending mass messages, for example, might be something you do just once every quarter. But the key is to focus on creating the most effective process that you will follow every day.

Decide how much time you can devote to your lead generation campaign **each day**, whether it is fifteen minutes, thirty minutes, or sixty minutes. Whatever it is, be consistent because the more consistent you are, the better your results will be.

Here is a sample checklist you can use to help create your own checklist.

Sample Daily LinkedIn Lead Generation Checklist

LinkedIn Daily/Weekly Task List
Daily
Post Status Update On Personal Profile & Company Page
Accept, Tag & Send Welcome Message To New Connections
Respond To New Messages
Send Connection Requests To People You Know Or Met
Connect With 5-10 New Potential Prospects
Send Relationship Building Messages & Set Follow Up Reminders
Review your Notifications & Home Page News Feed
Weekly
Find Content to Share
Post An Article Or Blog Post In Groups
Comment In LinkedIn Groups
Monthly
Give & Request Recommendations
Give Endorsements
As Necessary
Review Your LinkedIn Groups [add or delete groups]
Send Mass Messages

Remember, the sample provided above and the tasks and frequency listed within are just suggestions and guidelines to help you create your own checklist. Make sure that you take the time to personalize it to meet both your goals and the time you can dedicate to it. You will want to review this checklist a couple of times a year to make sure that each step is efficient and makes sense for you.

As you become more familiar and comfortable with this process, you may also find new ways of improving the efficiency of your checklist. If one or more of the steps is not producing results or doesn't work for your industry or goals, then you may want to remove it.

The key is to create a system and routine that becomes second nature in order to utilize this powerful lead generation tool to its full potential. I urge you to implement everything you are learning from this book—sharing great content, becoming an authority on your topic, growing your network, targeting specific prospects, staying organized, tagging, and adding notes and reminders. If you do this consistently, you will see amazing results in the form of more leads, more clients, and more revenue.

Here is a great example of the success you can have by creating and then following your checklist daily.

Social Selling Case Study 5 – Darrel Griffin of Social4Sales

www.linkedin.com/in/signageadviser

Darrel Griffin is a Western Australia-based Signage Adviser with over 20 years of experience in B2B sales, predominantly in the UK.

Due to the exceptional success of his social selling efforts, he has also launched a consultancy, Social4Sales, aimed at training fellow sales professionals in the art of social selling.

The Challenge

Prior to using social selling or LinkedIn, Darrel was selling using a combination of cold calling and email prospecting.

With little to no information about the companies he was contacting, he generally found himself resorting to calling the business to get the name and email address of the person he needed to contact from the gatekeeper. In the rare instances where this tactic did pay off, he would email the person and then follow up a few days later.

The process required a lot of time and work with a very low to moderate return. Darrel knew he needed to find a better way to prospect for new leads.

The Solution

Darrel moved to Western Australia with his family in 2012. Starting from scratch and with no professional connections, he decided to immerse himself in social media as a way to build business relationships. He decided to focus on LinkedIn in particular.

He created a plan and then over many hours created his personal brand and ensured his profiles were complete and up-to-date. He focused on connecting with professionals within his employers' target markets.

Each day he set aside time to post daily updates and interact with his ever-growing network, taking the time to capitalize on opportunities such as sending birthday greetings or congratulations to contacts with work anniversaries. He also took the time to read the posts and content of others and then "like", comment, or reply as appropriate. He also participated in many group conversations.

Darrel made a consistent effort to ensure that he was top of mind in his field. Gradually, he began to be invited to look at signage projects by his connections and by the end of the year, he saw remarkable results.

The Results

In 2013, 42% of the leads Darrel generated for his employers came directly from his LinkedIn activity, equating to over one million dollars worth of leads.

In one instance, after he had been connected to an advertising agency's Creative Director for some time, he was contacted via LinkedIn and asked if he'd like to come in and discuss a project. During the meeting, he was able to introduce new digital signage technologies which resulted in further presentations to the agency's entire staff and then to one of the agency's clients—a major prestige car manufacturer.

Takeaways

- Social selling isn't a magic bullet—it can be done badly and this can be seen every day.

- Social selling is first and foremost relational—it's SOCIAL media, not sales media.

- Social selling requires a long term approach and results are rarely immediate.

- Social selling does require a time investment but the ROI definitely justifies it.

- Social selling requires consistency.

- Social selling opens up doors that would otherwise be closed!

Darrel states:

"LinkedIn is a powerful tool, no doubt about it. In the right hands, it can definitely generate new business—I've proved that!"

Chapter 9: Creating Your Relationship Building Messages

Internalize the 'Golden Rule' of sales that says, 'All things being equal, people will do business with, and refer business to, those people they know, like and trust.'
~Bob Burg

As I mentioned in the etiquette and best practices section, when you connect with other people on LinkedIn, it is vital that you don't make the mistake most people make by using LinkedIn's default messages. These cold, impersonal messages do nothing to help create a real, personal connection with your potential prospects.

Instead, I recommend you personalize and customize your connection request messages for each person you connect with. To keep this from becoming too time-consuming, you can create a series of sample message scripts, which you can quickly choose from and use depending on the situation.

In this chapter, I will show you an example of the different types of message scripts introduced in Chapter 7. For each script, I will include the goal and how to structure each message.

So let's take a look at these messages that will make you a champion LinkedIn connection and relationship builder!

Connection Request Messages

There are several different scripts you will want to create to connect with people depending on how and why you have chosen to connect with that person. Keep in mind you have only **300 characters** to work with.

Fellow Group Members

Let's say, for example, you wanted to connect with someone who could be a potential prospect but you don't know this person. The best way to do this is to find a group that you both have in common and to mention that group in your message.

Here's an example of what this message might look like:

Hi < Insert Name >,

We are both members of < Insert Name of Group Here > and I thought it would be great to connect to share ideas, exchange information or just get to know about each other's work. I look forward to learning more about you.

Melonie Dodaro

Notice that your message should start by mentioning the group you both belong to as well as any other commonalities you can include such as similar location or industry.

Create your script below:

CONNECTION REQUEST MESSAGE [GROUP MEMBERS] – 300 CHARACTERS [MAX]

If You Do Not Share a Common Group

When you don't share a common group, your goal is to tell them why you want to connect and establish some commonality to start building rapport. If you share something in common, you will want to stress this in the message.

Here is an example of a message you can create:

Hi <Insert Name>,

I'd be honored to connect with you here on LinkedIn as I continue to expand my network with <name of your target market, e.g., professionals, business owners, accountants etc.>. I noticed we share some common interests. If there's anything I can do to support you, please feel free to contact me.

Melonie Dodaro

Create your script below:

CONNECTION REQUEST MESSAGE [DON'T KNOW & DON'T SHARE A COMMON GROUP – 300 CHARACTERS [MAX]

_____

_____

_____

_____

_____

_____

_____

_____

_____

_____

_____

Just Met

It's always a great idea to connect and stay in touch on LinkedIn with new people you've recently met. Start by reminding them of how you met, just in case they have forgotten where you met or who you are.

It can be as simple as this example:

Hi <Insert Name>,

It was great to meet you at the SOHO event in Toronto yesterday, and I would love to connect with you on LinkedIn. If there's anything I can do to support you, please don't hesitate to contact me.

Melonie Dodaro

Create your script below:

CONNECTION REQUEST MESSAGE [RECENTLY MET] – 300 CHARACTERS [MAX]

Welcome / Thank You Message

Once somebody has accepted your connection request or they have connected with you, it's a great idea to send what I call a welcome or thank you message.

The goal of this message is to start a dialogue. If you are building an email list, this is a great opportunity to get them to download a free report or something else that would be of value to them. It could be something connected to their industry, a report, a whitepaper, a link to a blog post, or a video—anything that they might find helpful. I often invite people to view a relevant article, download my LinkedIn Checklist, or watch a webinar that they might be interested in.

The goal of your Welcome Message is to start a dialogue and provide something of value or interest to them.

Here's an example of what this message might look like:

Hi < Insert Name >,

Thanks so much for connecting with me here on LinkedIn. I thought you'd find this article "5 Steps to Succeed with Social Selling On LinkedIn" interesting.

You can read it here: http://topdogsocialmedia.com/social-selling-on-linkedin/

There are some stats in the article you might find interesting, such as:

- *72.6% of salespeople who use social media outperform their colleagues that don't use it*

Let me know what you think about it.

Have a great day.

Melonie

Notice, I'm not trying to pitch anything. I'm just providing a nice friendly welcome message to build some rapport. Another approach you may want to take is to start a dialogue by asking them a question to learn more about them.

It is important to remember that even though you are creating a message script, you still have the opportunity to personalize the message with their name and anything else that would make the message more relevant to them. It's important that you take advantage of this and don't simply send a standard, generic message.

Create your script below:

WELCOME/THANK YOU MESSAGE

_____

_____

_____

_____

_____

_____

_____

_____

_____

Relationship Building Messages

If you are using LinkedIn as a business building tool, then establishing a strong relationship becomes extremely important.

One of the ways I do this is by sending a message to build the relationship and continue to add value about a week or so after connecting. I call this the Relationship Building Message.

Here is an example of what a relationship-building message may look like:

Hi <Insert Name>,

How are you?

I just created a new thirty-minute training video showing sales leaders and professionals how to leverage LinkedIn for lead generation. I thought I'd send it over to you in case you felt that your sales force could benefit from learning more about the power of social selling.

*The training is called **"Social Selling: 3 Steps To Get A Flood of Leads From LinkedIn"***

You are welcome to share this free training with your sales team.

To access this free training, go to

http://SocialSellingOnLinkedIn.com

If you have any questions or if there is something I can help you with, feel free to reach out to me.

Melonie

With this message I'm sending them a thirty-minute free training video and inviting them to share it with their sales force. Again, I'm not pitching anything, but I am positioning myself as someone who provides value and is an authority on Social Selling.

Create your script below:

RELATIONSHIP BUILDING MESSAGE

_____

_____

_____

_____

_____

_____

_____

_____

_____

_____

_____

_____

_____

_____

_____

_____

_____

_____

_____

_____

_____

_____

_____

_____

_____

_____

Move the Relationship off-line

One of the biggest mistakes I see people make with social media is continuing to maintain relationships strictly online. The only way to convert a prospect to a client is to move the relationship off-line.

You will want to create a second Relationship Building Message with this purpose in mind, to move the relationship off-line. You will typically send this message between one to four weeks after your last message and the goal is to set up a phone call, Skype call, or an in-person meeting, depending upon how you do business.

Here is an example of what a relationship-building message with the purpose of moving the relationship off-line may look like:

Hi <Insert Name>,

Hope you are doing well. I just wanted to follow up with you on the video training I shared with you a couple of weeks ago. Did you share that video with your sales team?

I wanted to find out if you had any questions about social selling and the impact on sales teams that effectively utilize it.

I'd be happy to schedule a time to chat about social selling best practices for your sales team. Are you available for a phone call next Tuesday or Thursday?

Let me know a couple of days and times that work for you and we can jump on a quick call.

Looking forward to hearing back from you.

Melonie

This message can be sent between one to four weeks after your last message, and you should set a reminder to send it with the Reminder feature in LinkedIn. This is your opportunity to move the relationship forward.

Create your script below:

RELATIONSHIP BUILDING MESSAGE – MOVING IT OFF-LINE

_____

_____

_____

_____

_____

_____

_____

_____

_____

_____

_____

_____

_____

Now that I've shown you the various scripts you will want to create for your lead generation campaign, it's time to complete your own, so you can put your plan on autopilot. Having these handy pre-written message scripts will streamline your efforts, save you time, and help you to grow a robust network of leads, prospects, and new clients.

I recommend you keep these messages in a text document on your computer where you can easily copy and paste the messages and tweak them as necessary every time you make a new connection.

Chapter 10: Do You Need a LinkedIn Premium Account?

"With a premium account, you can send InMails to reach anyone on LinkedIn, get hundreds of additional search results, and see more information about who's viewed your profile."
~LinkedIn Premium Help Center

There are a number of different types of paid LinkedIn accounts[32] available for those wishing to upgrade to a premium LinkedIn account. For most members that are considering upgrading, LinkedIn Premium is the most balanced paid account type and will generally suit most business owners and professionals.

The LinkedIn Premium Account has four different levels of membership that you can choose from depending on your budget and needs: Business, Business Plus, Executive and Pro. There are also premium versions specifically for recruiters and sales professionals.

While you may only ever need to use the free version of LinkedIn, there are three premium features that you may wish to consider upgrading to a paid account in order to use:

- Additional Advanced Search Functions

---

[32] LinkedIn paid account types include *LinkedIn Premium*, *For Recruiters*, *For Job Seekers* and *For Sales Professionals*

- Who's Viewed Your Profile
- InMail

Advanced Search

In the right-hand section of the Advanced Search there are eight Premium fields that are available to paid members. These are valuable because of their ability to help you narrow down and target your searches. While four of those fields are available only to the Executive and Pro Premium level members, the other four search fields are accessible to paid members with the Business or Business Plus level membership which includes the following search fields.

- **Company Size**: Allows you to target small businesses and freelancers (select the 1–10 option), very large businesses (select the 10,000+ option), or any size in between.

- **Seniority Level**: Allows you to narrow your search by seniority levels such as VP, Manager, Senior, Owner and Partner.

- **Interested In**: Allows you to choose from options such as Industry Experts, Entrepreneurs or Consultants/Contractors to look for specific groups of people.

- **Fortune 1000**: Allows you to limit your search for only employees at Fortune 1000 companies. There are a number of options that allow you to select from Fortune 50, Fortune 501–1000 and several choices in between. This search field is the most valuable of the four.

Let's say you are looking to connect with Communications VPs of Fortune 50 companies that you share a connection or group with. For this search, you would type "communications" in the **Keyword** field and select "Anywhere" under **Location**. Finally check "2nd Connections" and "Group Members" from **Relationship**, "VP" from **Seniority Level** and "Fortune 50" under the **Fortune 1000** section.

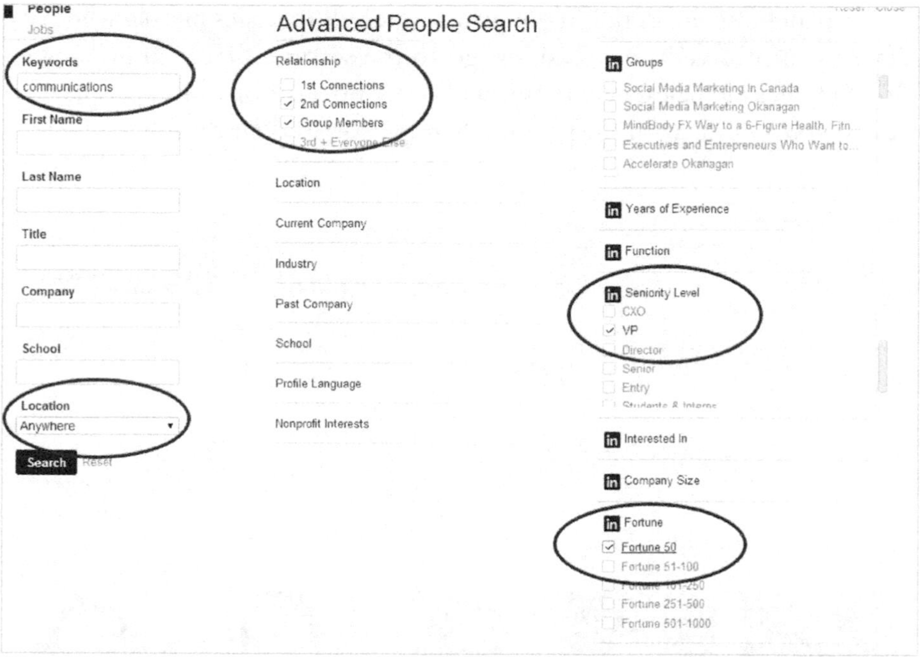

Image 10.1: You can further narrow your search results using the premium search fields.

Who's Viewed Your Profile?

An excellent source of potential connections can be found in your *Who's Viewed Your Profile* page. This page provides a list of people who have recently viewed your profile. While free members can only see the last five people to have viewed their profile, premium members get to see the full list of people from the last ninety days.

With the premium version of Who's Viewed Your Profile, you can view your search stats and even sort all the people who viewed your profile by industry, position, what company they work for, where they live, how they found your profile, and what type of keywords they used when searching.

The benefit of this is that if you want to see all the sales people who have viewed your profile, you would just go to the section "What Your Viewers Do" and click on Salesperson. This will bring up a list of all the people who viewed your profile with the position Salesperson in their profile.

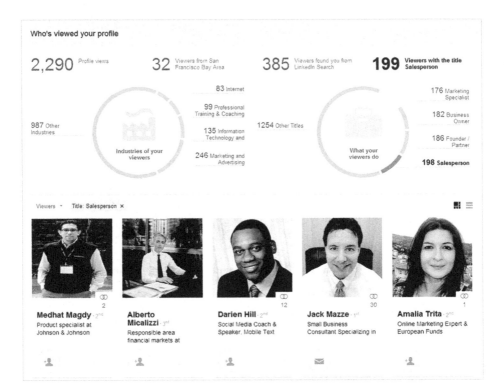

Image 10.2: Use the filter features in Who's Viewed my Profile to search for potential prospects.

InMail

These are messages you send directly within LinkedIn to another member whom you are not already connected with. You might choose to send these to people whom you would like to connect with before you send a LinkedIn

Connection Request to see if they'd be open to connecting with you on LinkedIn.

Using an InMail greatly increases your chances of success because they have a much higher open rate compared to that of email[33]. This improves your ability to talk to and connect directly with top decision makers. This feature also includes a guaranteed seven-day response rate. If the person you contacted doesn't contact you within seven days, LinkedIn will credit you with another InMail to send—even if the person you contacted replies to you after seven days.

While all members can purchase InMails, there are a number of benefits exclusive to Premium Members. As a Premium Member, you receive a number of free InMails each month[34], you can accumulate your InMail credits from month to month[35] and you can purchase up to 10 more InMails per month above what your account type allows.

---

[33] See LinkedIn Marketing Solutions CEB Case Study example http://marketing.linkedin.com/sites/default/files/pdfs/LinkedIn_CEB_CaseStudy2013.pdf
[34] The number of free InMails per month for paid members depends on which type of LinkedIn Premium Membership you buy
[35] InMail credits accumulated from month to month will expire after 90-days.

Chapter 11: Cracking the LinkedIn Code

"The art of simplicity is a puzzle of complexity".
~Douglas Horton

I have covered a lot of information in the book, so I have created a mnemonic which can be used to remind you how to crack the LinkedIn Code to generate more clients and sales for your business.

Here's how you can crack the:

LINKEDIN CODE

L - Listen

Listen to the language that your ideal clients use to describe their challenges and problems. This is the language you want to use in your profile and the messages you send.

I - Invest

Invest the time to complete your LinkedIn Profile. A fully completed and optimized profile will set you apart from your competitors.

N - Needs

Your profile, especially your headline and summary section, must speak to the **needs** of your ideal client; ensure it is client-focused.

K - Keywords

Make sure that you have used your **keywords** throughout your profile to ensure you show up at the top of LinkedIn search results.

E - Enhance

Visually **enhance** your profile by adding multi-media, such as videos, SlideShare presentations, and PDF documents.

D - Develop

Develop your LinkedIn lead generation campaign by creating a daily checklist and relationship-building messages you can put on autopilot.

I - Initiate

Initiate new relationships and dialogue by personalizing all of your messages, replies, and connection requests.

N - Nurture

Take the time to **nurture** your relationships on LinkedIn by creating a series of value-based messages.

C - Connect

Make an effort to regularly build your network and **connect** with new prospects and strategic partners. Your ability to find prospects or be found by those same prospects is limited to the size of your network.

O - Off-line

To move your relationship to the next level with a connection, you must move it **off-line**.

D - Dedicate

Dedicate at least thirty minutes a day to your LinkedIn campaign for the best results and you will see a dramatic increase in new leads, prospects, and clients.

E - Etiquette

Always make sure that you are following good LinkedIn **etiquette** and best practices.

Chapter 12: Final Thoughts: Cracking the LinkedIn Code

"With some focused prospecting activity, the results may be quicker than you think. As you develop your network, share worthwhile and valuable content, be memorable, and respond to contact and engagement opportunities, results will develop over time."
~Mark Stonham

The rules of marketing are changing and if you want to continue to bring in new clients and generate more sales, you need to change your marketing strategies as well.

Social selling works, not because it is a gimmick or a way to inundate your target market with your marketing message but rather because it is about creating personal relationships with your prospects that are built on trust. It is an ongoing process—just like any good relationship, it requires regular time and upkeep.

The benefit of this is that when these prospects are ready to buy, you will have positioned yourself as THE credible expert that they know, like, and trust. You have set yourself up as the first choice in their mind.

Before you begin the social selling process on LinkedIn, you must ensure that your profile is professional looking, optimized for searches, and that it speaks to your ideal clients.

You must also make sure that you understand and follow the best practices of LinkedIn. Failure to do so could mean consequences that range from annoying potential prospects to being restricted or removed from LinkedIn.

In preparation to begin the process of social selling, you need to create a daily action plan that you can follow as well as create a number of message scripts you can use to reach out and follow up with connections in a methodical and repeatable process. This plan will include only the highest yielding activities and should be tweaked on a regular basis to meet your company's individual needs.

It is my great hope that I have shown you the power and benefit of using LinkedIn for social selling and that I have laid out steps that are easy for you to understand and follow.

Let's Connect

I always enjoy hearing people's LinkedIn success stories, so please do write and tell me about yours at **info@topdogsocialmedia.com**—I might even write about it in one of my upcoming blog posts!

You can also connect with me on LinkedIn (**www.linkedin.com/in/meloniedodaro**), but be sure to write me a personalized message that mentions this book.

I wish you lots of success with your LinkedIn lead generation campaign!

About the Author

MELONIE DODARO is the founder of Top Dog Social Media, an agency that helps professionals and sales teams leverage social selling to boost their visibility, attract more leads and clients, and put more revenue in their pipeline.

She trains sales teams all across North America on how to use LinkedIn and on advanced social selling techniques. These are the same tactics being used by the biggest companies on the planet that have implemented social selling practices with outstanding results.

Melonie works with some of the country's largest media companies, financial services organizations, marketing companies, and logistics and leasing companies.

Some of Melonie's speaking appearances include:

- Social Media Marketing World in San Diego
- Social Media Camp, Canada's largest social media conference
- Franchise annual conferences
- Industry, trade and corporate events

She has been dubbed by the media as Canada's #1 LinkedIn expert. Melonie is known worldwide for her LinkedIn and social selling expertise. Other social media experts come to her for advice, training, and help with all things LinkedIn related.

Social Media Examiner listed her blog as one of the Top 10 Social Media Blogs worldwide in 2014.

Connect With Me On Social Media

ⓘ   http://www.linkedin.com/in/MelonieDodaro

ⓘ   https://www.facebook.com/TopDogSocialMedia

ⓘ   https://twitter.com/MelonieDodaro

ⓘ   http://www.pinterest.com/MelonieDodaro

ⓘ   https://www.youtube.com/user/TopDogSocialMedia

ⓘ   https://plus.google.com/+MelonieDodaro

ⓘ   http://TopDogSocialMedia.com/blog/

The LinkedIn Code – Bonus Master Class

Want to learn how to implement what you just read?

Your copy of this book is your ticket to an exciting NEW presentation that solidifies the information in this book. Turn yourself (or your organization) into a Social Selling MACHINE with the exclusive tactics shared in this training. During the FREE sixty-minute Master Class you will discover:

- **How to leverage the power of social selling to generate more leads and clients!** (This is the same lead generation tactic that I've used for the past three years to double my business year over year and you can get the same kind of results if you just follow the steps!)

- **The secret structure that makes your profile stand out from the competition and practically FORCES your ideal prospect to contact you.** (You'll discover the ONE THING you must include in your profile if you wish your prospects to get in touch with you)

- **The 7 biggest mistakes OTHERS make on LinkedIn that can damage their credibility.** After this webinar, you'll NEVER make these mistakes again! (Sounds boring, but if you don't follow these tips, you risk being blocked or restricted by LinkedIn and never contacted for lucrative deals!)

- **The "Social Selling Formula" NOBODY else uses and turns prospects into clients faster than you can pick up the phone!** This is SO powerful, I usually reserve this for my highest paying clients. If you take nothing else away from this webinar, be sure to take this! Your business could literally explode overnight once you use this proven formula.

- **The proven three-step formula only the top 1% of LinkedIn experts use to connect with decision makers.** Follow these steps and you'll have an endless list of high quality prospects that want what you offer and are willing to listen to you.

To register for this free Master Class go to:

http://LICodeWebinar.com

Social Selling Training for Sales Teams

Attention Sales Trainers, Sales Managers and VPs:

Is your organization repositioned to take advantage of the shift away from traditional selling to the new social selling methods?

Are you taking advantage of the power of social media tools, such as LinkedIn, to help your sales force meet their objectives month after month, year after year?

Or are you watching your competitors steal market share, clients and—most importantly—profits because they're already connecting with the best prospects using these tools?

Social selling is a relationship-building process and this book shows you how you'll get much better results than cold calling or door knocking.

Imagine having your sales professionals easily reach key decision makers and prospects faster and with a higher degree of success. One of the best parts about using LinkedIn for prospecting is that almost EVERY decision maker, regardless of their position, manages their own LinkedIn account. This means your people can easily bypass any gatekeepers and connect directly with the people who are in a position to hear their sales story.

> **FACT: 72.6% of salespeople who use social media outperform their colleagues that aren't using it.**

If your goal is to shorten your sales cycle, have your sales people spend more time in front of key decision makers, and ultimately close more business, then connect with me to learn more about the social selling training programs I run specifically for sales teams. Your sales teams will get the same methods that my colleagues and I have used to train companies such as Oracle, IBM, American Express, ADP and many others. It is the most robust and effective social selling training that exists in the marketplace.

Here are just some examples of the training modules that we offer:

- Creating a client-focused, buyer-centric, LinkedIn profile
- Mapping out your buyers' personas
- Finding content that intrigues your buyer
- Prospecting and connecting with buyers on LinkedIn
- Sphere of influence selling
- Creating a social selling daily routine
- Top social selling strategies
- LinkedIn etiquette & best practices

Our advanced social selling curriculum will have your sales people working more effectively, more efficiently, and earning more money for themselves and for your company. Imagine how much happier your office will be when everyone is meeting or exceeding quota.

Top social selling companies or sales teams

- Are 36% more likely than the average sales team to achieve their quota.
- Consistently see a 12.2% higher year-over-year increase in total company revenue.
- See a 7.2% higher year-over-year increases in the average deal size or contract value.

If you have any questions about our social selling training to help your sales team master this new way of selling, just reach out to us directly at **info@ topdogsocialmedia.com**.

Cracking The LinkedIn Code: Melonie's High Performance LinkedIn Training

If You're Not Using LinkedIn to Grow Your Business,
You're Missing Out on a Veritable Flood of New Leads, Clients
and Higher Profits

LinkedIn is the LARGEST, MOST TARGETED database of business owners, managers and decision makers in the world and you NEED to be there. But – as with everything – there's a RIGHT way and a WRONG way to access this powerful business social network.

This book has given you an inside taste of what's possible with LinkedIn. But, a book has limitations and can only contain so much information.

That's why I've created an advanced online training program to give you all that you need to implement a profitable lead generation plan using LinkedIn.

Cracking The LinkedIn Code is the most up-to-date program on how to become the go-to person in your niche and create a massive business from your LinkedIn connections.

You'll walk away with the skills to:

- Quickly and easily connect with the decision makers in the companies you want to work with (no more awkward conversations with the gatekeeper – or landing in the dreaded "voice mail jail" where no one ever returns your calls)

- Create your own personal lead list of people who will automatically trust you (Hint: your profile is an outstanding place for people to get to know you, like you and trust you before you ever connect with them)

- Use LinkedIn as a contact management tool where you can easily keep track of contacts, correspondence, phone conversations and more

- Have people eager to receive your marketing messages, connect with you and ask for your products or services (This is so powerful, I don't even share it with most of my personal clients, but it slipped out when I was recording the course so it's "out there" for you too.)

- Most importantly – how to do all of the above – and a lot more – without coming across as desperate, needy, or worse, the epitome of a '70's used car salesman

- And much more!

Each module is carefully crafted to build on the one before it and once you've completed the course you'll be ahead of 97.3% of all LinkedIn users – and almost ALL your competitors!

The best part is you can take this at your own leisure. It's on-line and self-directed. You could finish it in a few days or a few weeks, whatever works best for you. (The faster you complete the course the sooner you could be growing your business!)

Learn more about this advanced training at: **http://LICodeProgram.com**

References

[1] Jason Miller, "The Sophisticated Marketer's Guide to LinkedIn," January, 2014, **http://marketing.linkedin.com/blog/introducing-the-sophisticated-marketers-guide-to-linkedin/**):

[2] Aberdeen Group, "Social Selling: Leveraging the Power of User-Generated Content to Optimize Sales Results," February 2013. **http://www.slideshare.net/linkedin-sales-solutions/social-selling-impact-aberdeen-report-2013**

[3] Sergey Gusarov, "Social Selling Facts," Jan 21, 2013 **http://www.slideshare.net/sergeygusarov165/social-selling-facts**

[4] Tom Martin, "Sales Strategies to Sell to Self Educated BtoB Buyers," January 24, 2013. **http://www.conversedigital.com/sales-prospecting/selling-to-the-self-educated-b-to-b-buyer**

[5] Meghan Keaney Anderson, "The 5 Social Media Metrics Your CEO Actually Cares About," May 29, 2013 **http://blog.hubspot.com/marketing/social-media-metrics-ceos-cares-about**

[6] Rebecca Corliss, "LinkedIn 277% More Effective for Lead Generation Than Facebook & Twitter," January 30, 2012 **http://blog.hubspot.com/blog/tabid/6307/bid/30030/LinkedIn-277-More-Effective-for-Lead-Generation-Than-Facebook-Twitter-New-Data.aspx**

[7] Scott Logan (Marketing Campaign Manager) from InContact **http://www.incontact.com/**

[8] Deep Nishar, "The Evolution of LinkedIn: Slide Show," 2013 **http://blog.linkedin.com/2013/05/06/the-evolution-of-linkedin/**

[9] Steve Olsher, "Internet Prophets: The World's Leading Experts Reveal How to Profit Online", 2012, chapter 10 pp112-113 **http:// internetprophets.com/DL/Internet-Prophets.pdf**

Index

T

V

W

Y